TROUBLE

at the TOP

The Nonprofit Board's Guide to Managing an Imperfect Chief Executive

Katha Kissman

BOARDSOURCE®
Building Effective Nonprofit Boards

Library of Congress Cataloging-in-Publication Data

Kissman, Katha

   Trouble at the top : the nonprofit board's guide to managing an
      imperfect chief executive / Katha Kissman.

      p. cm. --

   ISBN 1-58686-112-3

   1. Nonprofit organizations--Management. 2. Chief executive officers.
   3. Boards of directors. 4. Directors of corporations. I. Title.

   HD62.6.K539 2009

      658.4'07--dc22   2009029390

© 2009 BoardSource.
First Printing, September 2009
ISBN 1-58686-112-3

Published by BoardSource
1828 L Street, NW, Suite 900
Washington, DC 20036

BoardSource is dedicated to advancing the public good by building exceptional nonprofit boards and inspiring board service.

BoardSource was established in 1988 by the Association of Governing Boards of Universities and Colleges (AGB) and Independent Sector (IS). Prior to this, in the early 1980s, the two organizations had conducted a survey and found that although 30 percent of respondents believed they were doing a good job of board education and training, the rest of the respondents reported little, if any, activity in strengthening governance. As a result, AGB and IS proposed the creation of a new organization whose mission would be to increase the effectiveness of nonprofit boards.

With a lead grant from the Kellogg Foundation and funding from five other donors, BoardSource opened its doors in 1988 as the National Center for Nonprofit Boards with a staff of three and an operating budget of $385,000. On January 1, 2002, BoardSource took on its new name and identity. These changes were the culmination of an extensive process of understanding how we were perceived, what our audiences wanted, and how we could best meet the needs of nonprofit organizations.

Today, BoardSource is the premier voice of nonprofit governance. Its highly acclaimed products, programs, and services mobilize boards so that organizations fulfill their missions, achieve their goals, increase their impact, and extend their influence. BoardSource is a 501(c)(3) organization.

BoardSource provides

- resources to nonprofit leaders through workshops, training, and an extensive Web site (www.boardsource.org)

- governance consultants who work directly with nonprofit leaders to design specialized solutions to meet an organization's needs

- the world's largest, most comprehensive selection of material on nonprofit governance, including a large selection of books and CD-ROMs

- an annual conference that brings together approximately 900 governance experts, board members, and chief executives and senior staff from around the world

For more information, please visit our Web site at www.boardsource.org, e-mail us at mail@boardsource.org, or call us at 800-883-6262.

Have You Used These BoardSource Resources?

THE GOVERNANCE SERIES

1. *Ten Basic Responsibilities of Nonprofit Boards, Second Edition*
2. *Legal Responsibilities of Nonprofit Boards, Second Edition*
3. *Financial Responsibilities of Nonprofit Boards, Second Edition*
4. *Fundraising Responsibilities of Nonprofit Boards, Second Edition*
5. *The Nonprofit Board's Role in Mission, Planning, and Evaluation, Second Edition*
6. *Structures and Practices of Nonprofit Boards, Second Edition*

BOOKS

The Board Chair Handbook, Second Edition

Getting the Best from Your Board: An Executive's Guide to a Successful Partnership

Taming the Troublesome Board Member

Moving Beyond Founder's Syndrome to Nonprofit Success

Chief Executive Transitions: How to Hire and Support a Nonprofit CEO

Chief Executive Succession Planning: The Board's Role in Securing Your Organization's Future

Assessment of the Chief Executive

Culture of Inquiry: Healthy Debate in the Boardroom

Governance as Leadership: Reframing the Work of Nonprofit Boards

Understanding Nonprofit Financial Statements, Third Edition

The Nonprofit Board Answer Book: A Practical Guide for Board Members and Chief Executives, Second Edition

The Board Building Cycle: Nine Steps to Finding, Recruiting, and Engaging Nonprofit Board Members, Second Edition

Navigating the Organizational Lifecycle: A Capacity-Building Guide for Nonprofit Leaders

The Nonprofit Dashboard: A Tool for Tracking Progress

Financial Committees

The Nonprofit Legal Landscape

The Nonprofit Board's Guide to Bylaws

Managing Conflicts of Interest: A Primer for Nonprofit Boards, Second Edition

The Nonprofit Policy Sampler, Second Edition

The Source: Twelve Principles of Governance That Power Exceptional Boards

Fearless Fundraising for Nonprofit Boards, Second Edition

Driving Strategic Planning: A Nonprofit Executive's Guide

Who's Minding the Money? An Investment Guide for Nonprofit Board Members, Secoond Edition

DVDs

Meeting the Challenge: An Orientation to Nonprofit Board Service

Speaking of Money: A Guide to Fundraising for Nonprofit Board Members

ONLINE ASSESSMENTS

Board Self-Assessment

Assessment of the Chief Executive

Executive Search — Needs Assessment

For an up-to-date list of publications and information about current prices, membership, and other services, please call BoardSource at 800-883-6262 or visit our Web site at www.boardsource.org . For consulting services, please e-mail us at consulting@boardsource.org or call 877-892-6293.

CONTENTS

ACKNOWLEDGMENTS **1**

FOREWORD **3**

INTRODUCTION **5**
Who Can Benefit from This Book 5
Stories from the Field 6
The Structure of This Book 7

SECTION 1: *NONALIGNMENT WITH BOARD, STAFF, OR ORGANIZATION NEEDS* **9**
#1: Failing to Integrate into or Respect Organizational Culture 9
#2: All Vision and No Process 11
#3: All Process and No Vision 13
#4: Failing to Use the Board 14
#5: Creating Cliques and Group Divisions 16
#6: Criticizing the Organization in Public 19

SECTION 2: *INCOMPETENCE* **23**
#7: Impulsivity or Financial Recklessness 23
#8: Resisting New Opportunities 25

SECTION 3: *INSUBORDINATION* **27**
#9:   No Follow-Through on Promises to the Board 27
#10: Undermining the Board Chair 28
#11: Not Keeping the Board Informed 29
#12: Acting without Authority 30
#13: Missing Established Goals 32
#14: Deviating from Policy 33
#15: Deviating from the Mission 34
#16: Failing to Stick to a Budget 35

SECTION 4: *ILLEGAL OR UNETHICAL BEHAVIOR* **37**
#17: Lying 37
#18: Seeking or Receiving Inappropriate Financial Return from
        Outside Affiliations 39
#19: Engaging in Illegal Activity 40

SECTION 5: *MANAGEMENT STYLE AND PERSONAL ISSUES* **43**
#20: Staff Is Coming Directly to the Board with Concerns 43
#21: Bullying or Displaying a Controlling Personality 46
#22: Exhibiting Emotional Issues and Dependency 48

SECTION 6: *THE BASICS: GETTING THE BEST FROM YOUR CHIEF EXECUTIVE* **51**
The Search Process and the Board's Responsibility for Due Diligence 51
Hiring: Getting the Right Candidate for the Right Reasons 54
Proper Onboarding and Orientation 55
Confirming Who's the Boss 57
Delegation of Authority 57
Establishing a Proper Chief Executive Evaluation 58
Punitive Evaluations 61

CONCLUSION: *WE'RE ONLY HUMAN* **63**
Holding up the Mirror 63
Good Night and Good Luck 64

APPENDIX: *GRANTING AUTHORITY TO THE CHIEF EXECUTIVE: A TEMPLATE* **67**

SUGGESTED RESOURCES **69**

ABOUT THE AUTHOR **73**

ACKNOWLEDGMENTS

I wish to thank the numerous individuals who have helped me in my research and brainstorming about this topic.

Special thanks to the team at BoardSource, especially Karen Hansen, Outi Flynn, and Danielle Henry. Their unfailing good cheer combined with their incredible knowledge made this a wonderful return engagement.

This text builds on my previous BoardSource publication, *Taming the Troublesome Board Member*. In addition, I wish to thank the authors of BoardSource's many publications; in particular, *Getting the Best from Your Board* and *Moving Beyond Founder's Syndrome to Nonprofit Success*. These two publications provide a fountain of information for anyone truly wishing to create a team spirit toward mission fulfillment.

And to those others I am grateful to have met and known in the human journey, who gave freely of time, insights, stories, and help: Marilyn Alexander, Gayle Anderson, Stephen N. Anderson, Mike Bell, Suzanne Bissell, Bobbi Blok, Marla Bobowick, Barkley Calkins, Mike Cherry, Bridget Cohee, Jane Cohen, Michael Daigneault, Jim Doti, Jacqueline Gilbert, Mary Gray, Ron Farina, Lyle Hanna, Joyce Henderson, Julie Hertzog, Karin Hollerbach, Catherine Irwin, Tom Jacobson, Larry Klinger, the late George Knight, Bob Langert, The Honorable Al Lenhardt, Bruce Lesley, Marcia Lipetz, Debra Liverpool, Sally McConnell-Ginet, J. Schuyler Morgan, Bill Musick, Naomi Naierman, Esther Newman, Eliot Pfanstiehl, Lana Porter, Alyson Reed, Karen Rice, Lucia Riddle, Carolyn Saxton, Michelle Skaff, Jeffrey Slavin, Doug Sokolosky, Valerie Sokolosky, Ellen Solomon, Jeffrey Slavin, David Styers, Larry Vellani, Gregory Ward, Jerry Whiddon, and those several others who asked to remain anonymous.

I dedicate this book to my parents, Alvin and Nadra Kissman. How they have lived their lives, individually and together, has always given me inspirational guidance. I aspire daily to be like them. Thank you.

Finally, as before, I offer: No one is perfect. No one gets it right every time. But it is in the trying, the learning of lessons, the exchange of kindness, and the celebrating of successes together that the world is made better.

May it be so.

FOREWORD

The General Board of Pension and Health Benefits is an agency of The United Methodist Church, governed by a diverse group of 32 volunteer board members who are a microcosm of the Church itself. As with any organization, good governance and leadership are keys to our success. In order for our agency to maximize the value of our board's unique perspectives and collective opinions, we must develop a robust relationship with and among our board members — and between the board chair and the chief executive. The result is a strong group dynamic, invaluable to the decision making required for 74,000 retirement plan participants and the billions in assets we manage on their behalf.

For this reason, we are pleased to share our thoughts on the value this book may have for you and the considerations that brought us to work with Katha Kissman in 2008, as we planned to train our board for a new four-year cycle.

Education and training are the foundation for service on our board and we worked closely with Katha to provide a review of Policy Governance® principles and to examine the roles and responsibilities of our board members. With our new board, we devoted our very first meeting to paying particular attention to board governance instruction and explanation, so everyone would be on the same page from the outset, sharing an understanding for the particular structures and language we use.

We also put a great deal of emphasis on communications. In conjunction with BoardSource, we established an online Board of Directors' communications Web site for document sharing, meeting planning, virtual discussions, and online board meeting facilitation. Each of our board members brings a unique perspective and personal style, so we feel it is important for our board to speak freely, openly, and frequently. The recommendations Katha shared with us helped orchestrate a collegial dialogue aimed at building and preserving the relationships that make the board a cohesive working body.

We think you will see the benefit in Katha's approach to nonprofit boards and the working relationships required — we have even flipped it around a bit. While the relationship of a new chief executive to a board is critical, we also feel the relationship of a well-established chief executive to a new board is equally critical and we think you will find the suggestions contained here can flow both ways.

In this book Katha also identifies several ways these important relationships can falter, and she provides thoughtful considerations on rectifying them, including identifying when it is simply time to end the relationship. However, if you read this book in advance, it can be of particular value to those entering into a board chair or chief executive relationship for the first time because, as she illustrates, many problems are more easily avoided with advance planning and forethought and, in our opinion, a measure of foresight!

Group dynamics being what they are, we recognize that every board is different — it is difficult to legislate a one-size-fits-all approach to governance. While there are many ways to sustain a positive relationship, it does not happen by accident; it requires excellent communication and unwavering attention from all parties involved. But having worked closely with Katha, we feel you will find her thought-provoking scenarios can help you analyze the roles and responsibilities of your board chair, chief executive, and/or board members in order to identify and evaluate their actions. The payoff is an ongoing collaboration that delivers successful working relationships to benefit your organization.

We feel strongly that the special relationship between the board chair and the chief executive is one of the most important for the health of any organization and critical to good governance. Our comments are delivered jointly here because we enjoy and endorse a balanced working relationship as board chair and agency chief executive. We find that when you are working in tandem, your relationship becomes one of catalyst and conduit, as well as captain, coach, timekeeper, and referee.

The investment in relationship-building is what makes service on a not-for-profit board respectable, acceptable, collegial, and productive...and makes it all worthwhile.

Bishop B. Michael Watson
Board Chairperson

Barbara A. Boigegrain
CEO and General Secretary

INTRODUCTION

Supporting and evaluating the chief executive is perhaps the most important responsibility of the board of a nonprofit organization. And yet few resources exist to help nonprofit boards strengthen their relationship with the chief executive and respond to problems in that relationship as they arise.

While there are many books on evaluating chief executive and employee performance and on managing employees, this book addresses the nonprofit board's specific relationship to its chief executive.

How should volunteer boards deal appropriately with their unique and critical relationship with the chief executive? Where can they find guidance that is specific and consistent with the nature of the nonprofit sector and the board's governance role? How do they know what is required and when — gentle coaching, firm directive, or action and documentation for possible termination?

This book attempts to answer these questions by providing boards with guidance on how to handle specific issues that may arise in the board–chief executive relationship. Nonprofit boards often are a collective of disparate individuals who come to the table with varying communication skills and styles; varying levels of personal interest and experience; and varying opinions, perceptions, and perspectives. As a result, boards do not always have a shared sense of how best to manage and support the chief executive *as a team*, especially at times when a chief executive's behavior is compromising the effectiveness of the organization.

WHO CAN BENEFIT FROM THIS BOOK

As a companion publication to the BoardSource publications *Taming the Troublesome Board Member*, *Getting the Best from Your Board*, and *Moving Beyond Founder's Syndrome to Nonprofit Success*, this text provides tips, tools, and strategies for dealing with board–chief executive relationship challenges and opportunities.

The main audience for this book is the nonprofit board. Perhaps your board is seeking advice on how to start a new board–chief executive relationship off on the right foot. Maybe you need some ideas about how to address the effects of a specific situation, misunderstanding, failure to communicate, or other relationship challenge between a board and the chief executive. It is the author's fervent hope that board chairs in particular will find this book empowering and accessible, as they are the ones who need to initiate and facilitate action on behalf of a board.

This is not to say that this book can't be helpful for those who do not serve on nonprofit boards. Nonprofit consultants, for example, may find insights that will help them address challenging board–chief executive situations or relationships. And chief executives themselves may gain from this book a fuller understanding of certain challenges or problems relating to their relationship with their boards.

But it is the board that has the most to gain from these pages. This book should serve as a timely reminder that the board should pay close attention to its relationship with the chief executive. That relationship will be successful to the extent that there is open and transparent communication between the two parties — and to the extent that the board is able to recognize, intervene, and find the right path to follow in challenging situations.

Therefore, the book is organized as a reference guide to provide ready access to information about specific situations that might arise in the board–chief executive relationship. Reading the book from cover to cover in one sitting, while flattering to the author, is not advised. Rather, the author hopes and trusts that readers will find situations that resemble some of the challenges they face in their organizations — and gain new wisdom about how to handle those situations in ways that will benefit the organization, or at least result in only a minimal amount of damage.

STORIES FROM THE FIELD

The stories (real names have been changed) illustrate situations that may happen in the board–chief executive relationship in which problems or difficulties result from something that has happened or something that has failed to operate as it should. At the extreme, these issues could be problems of malfeasance, or could result in arguments, fighting, or violence. Certain issues can cause distress, worry, or anxiety, serving as a red flag that might require attention or intervention. In any event, if these actions or behaviors are not appropriately addressed, they can escalate from being temporary to chronic or mild and just plain irritating to serious enough to cause great and lasting damage.

The short- or long-term effects of a dysfunctional board–chief executive relationship can be one of the greatest detriments to any organization. These effects can be both direct — confusion, loss of energy or focus, difficulty in making decisions — and indirect — weakened morale, loss of productivity and service quality — and in extreme cases, cause high board or staff turnover, a damaged public reputation, or organizational financial instability.

The first step in finding a successful resolution to difficulties with an individual is recognizing that a person's actions or behaviors usually stem from something specific, whether it is ignorance, misunderstanding, a personality conflict, or a deeper issue. This is predicated on the assumption that a second step will occur — that leadership will intervene directly, humanely, with unity, and in a timely way. If leadership doesn't guide the process, trouble could be left unattended and may result in disaster. The final step, finding a winning solution, will require unique approaches for different groups and various answers for differing circumstances. In some cases it may involve looking at communication patterns and organizational processes, or require a major culture shift of both board and chief executive. And in still other cases, it will necessitate "holding up the mirror" to help the individual take a step back and understand the effects of his or her behavior within the context of the organization's work, and provide suggestions for change. And yes, the ultimate solution might also mean making a change in the person sitting in the chief executive position.

The board–chief executive relationship is about personal dynamics. No one enjoys conflict or confrontation, especially with regard to a professional colleague. Successfully working in a group context is highly dynamic and can engender great passion and emotion when disagreements or conflicts erupt. Paying attention to these dynamics and actively honoring the human element requires commitment and work. M. Scott Peck, M.D., in *The Road Less Traveled* (Touchstone, 2003) reminds us:

> *That process of confronting and solving problems is a painful one. Problems, depending upon their nature, evoke in us frustration or grief or sadness or loneliness or guilt or regret or anger or fear or anxiety or anguish or despair. These are uncomfortable feelings.... Fearing the pain involved, almost all of us, to a greater or lesser degree, attempt to avoid problems. We procrastinate, hoping that they will go away. We ignore them, forget them, pretend they do not exist.... We attempt to skirt around problems rather than meet them head on.*

Effective communication and positive conflict resolution are easiest to achieve when people treat each other with dignity and respect. It is under this overarching concept that this text provides strategies, tips, and tools to build an understanding of how to deal with certain common issues that may arise from the board–chief executive relationship.

THE STRUCTURE OF THIS BOOK

The stories in this book use the following general template to illustrate a wide variety of situations and offers recommendations to enhance a positive board–chief executive relationship:

- What's wrong

- Why this is a problem

- Case

- What could have been done differently

- What to do now

The book also includes after-the-fact conversation starters for some of the case studies to provide board members with ideas about the tone they may want to take in their conversations with chief executives about these issues.

In addition, throughout the book, the author provides quotes and other reminders in sidebars for the reader to ponder.

The book concludes with a section that focuses on the best way to avoid problems in the first place: Hire the right chief executive by engaging in a thoughtful, planned process involving the entire board. Then conduct orientation to get the chief executive off on the right foot and eventually a performance evaluation to ensure that feedback flows in both directions.

SECTION 1

NONALIGNMENT WITH BOARD, STAFF, OR ORGANIZATION NEEDS

What happens when the new chief executive just doesn't "fit"? Or when he or she paints a huge picture for the future but can't seem to make it happen? Or the exact opposite? Sometimes a chief executive either can't or won't use the time, talent, and treasure of the board. This section addresses these and a few other aspects that may arise when there is a disconnect between the staff leader and the organization.

#1: FAILING TO INTEGRATE INTO OR RESPECT ORGANIZATIONAL CULTURE

What's wrong: Sometimes a candidate can have all the right qualifications on paper, present herself outstandingly well in an interview, have impeccable references, but after she takes the job, it is clear that her style, temperament, and/or other aspects simply are not compatible with organizational culture and need.

Why this is a problem: A new chief executive has an opportunity to scan the cultural landscape of the organization he is joining and to integrate, take stock, and then proceed with changes after building team morale and consensus. Failure to do so may create unnecessary friction with staff members, board members, and/or other stakeholders. If the board does not acknowledge the situation quickly and try to either make it a good fit or to make a change, an organization can quickly lose ground.

Case: The Sunny Day Preschool was a somewhat large nonprofit that supported preschool children and had a policy of providing support for stay-at-home parents. The previous chief executive had been there for years. She was well-respected, had a lot of relevant experience, and she only left because her family was relocating.

The board hired a new person who had a strong educational background, but she was very cerebral — everything was theoretical and academic to her. She spent too much time talking and not enough time in action. In addition, her personal presentation was formal and impressive, while the staff was pretty casual and laid back. Part of this was due to the fact that salaries were not very high; staff didn't have a lot of money to spend on clothes. She often wore very expensive suits and accessories and sometimes it appeared that she was looking down at staff members who dressed more casually, despite the fact that there wasn't a dress code policy.

She did not relate well to the staff or to parents. Soon she made recommendations to the board about changes such as restructuring program initiatives, but she didn't get buy-in from the staff. While the board approved it, the staff mutinied. They were so upset that they went to the newspapers, expressing concern about what the potential impact on their clients would be.

The board sent a representative to the organization's major funders to let them know that the story would be in the paper. The funders asked the board what it was going to do about the conflict in the organization, and it was clear that the board didn't have a plan. As a result, the organization lost this and other funding. The historic major funders called for a meeting with the board and provided it with some action steps, one of which was to remove the chief executive (she resigned before any action was taken). The funders agreed to provide bridge funding but also insisted upon requirements for stricter monitoring of the organization's efforts.

The major funder: "This wasn't a situation where the previous chief executive controlled the board; rather, it was a weak board that had been carried by the previous chief executive. When she left, things began to fall apart — the new chief executive could not carry the board. Board members had never gone through a leadership transition and they didn't know what they didn't know. And the new chief executive was simply a poor choice."

What could have been done differently: The board had an opportunity to do a greater assessment of organizational need prior to conducting the chief executive search. In addition, boards in general may wish to probe more deeply into organizational culture so they understand how a potential candidate prefers to work, and how that fits (or doesn't) with the organization's prevailing style. Executive transition is not just about finding an executive who fits the current and future demands of the job (although it does that, too); it also focuses on minimizing the risk and capturing all of the opportunities that a change in leadership offers. A board has the opportunity to think ahead and actually make decisions and put into place what will need to happen when a CEO departs. This should be done while the chief executive is in place, to maximize timeliness and efficiency and minimize organizational trauma in the case of either planned or unplanned leadership turnover.

What to do now: In addition to the transition advice above, this board would benefit from training on or a review of board roles and responsibilities in order to increase its understanding of and effectiveness in its governance and oversight job.

NECESSARY KNOWLEDGE

APPRECIATIVE INQUIRY

The traditional approach to change is to look for the problem, do a diagnosis, and find a solution. The primary focus is on what is wrong or broken; since we look for problems, we find them. By paying attention to problems, we emphasize and amplify them.... Appreciative Inquiry suggests that we look for what works in an organization. The tangible result of the inquiry process is a series of statements that describe where the organization wants to be, based on the high moments of where they have been. Because the statements are grounded in real experience and history, people know how to repeat their success.

Source: *The Thin Book of Appreciative Inquiry, Second Edition* by Sue Hammond (Thin Book Publishing Company, 1998).

#2: ALL VISION AND NO PROCESS

What's wrong: The chief executive is a big-picture, future-oriented person coming up with lots of ideas, but who has no ability to make things happen (i.e., to begin and manage process).

Why this is a problem: Every organization wants a chief executive with vision — someone who can uncover hidden potential, find new possibilities for people and the organization, break new ground, and improve things through evolution. Just as important, however, organizations need chief executives who are able to supervise process. Good management and process skills enable a chief executive to achieve mission fulfillment by organizing logically, coordinating the work of different parties, taking a systematic approach, using agreed processes, and making and following plans. When a chief executive has limited abilities in the process area, the operations of an organization can quickly spiral out of control.

Case: Action for Children NOW! hired Susie Ryman as its new chief executive because she wowed the board at her interview. She had incredible ideas for taking the organization to greater heights — moving it from an organization with a wonderful program to one that would be center stage internationally with a strong advocacy capacity and a multitude of programs.

Less than two years later, however, it was clear that Ryman wasn't paying attention to the organization's infrastructure. While she was very good at creating connections and goodwill for the organization, back at the office, staff was floundering and the chief financial officer was very concerned about making payroll. Ryman didn't quite see the connection between spending and fiscal compliance, preferring her external role as a mover and shaker to her internal role as a manager and steward of the organization's finances and operations.

What could have been done differently: For most nonprofits, chief executives need to be brilliant internally as well as externally — masterfully stewarding all of the organization's resources while networking constantly to position the organization optimally with constituents, colleagues, funders, legislators, the media, and other audiences. In this case, the hiring process should have been structured to provide the board with assurance that candidates represented a good balance between vision and process skills, and to illuminate their key strengths and weaknesses. If a chief executive is only strong externally, then the board must ensure that there is a very strong chief operating officer or chief financial officer to focus on internal matters.

What to do now: The board needs to ensure that the organization is paying attention to internal as well as external priorities. This means engaging Ryman in a serious conversation about her ability (or lack thereof) to manage the organization successfully. If she affirms that this is indeed a problem for her, the board has a number of options. It can provide Ryman with the training and coaching she needs to manage the organization successfully, it can expand the role of the chief financial officer to pick up the slack, or it can seek a new executive who offers a better balance of process and vision.

The board also should consider implementing reporting mechanisms so that it can better monitor the organization's internal functions and head off any repeat of the problem in the future.

GET THE BEST FROM YOUR CHIEF EXECUTIVE

As a CEO, I want and need board members who are committed to the organization and its mission. I also want and need board members who have a bottom-line understanding. I need to be able to call on different board members at different times for different expertise — a diverse board that can help. And if they can't, to help me find others who can. I also want and need board members who are strong fundraisers. Individuals who will help me identify people that we can go to as potential donors, who are willing and able, after some training, to set up cultivation/ask appointments; and who are willing to accompany me on those visits. Board members need to understand that while there are different roles for board and staff, they are entangled roles that are required to work; even when there is disagreement, to be able to walk away and say we will still come together and work through the difficult issues together. And finally, board members who understand when it is time to make a change.

Carolyn Saxton
Executive Director
The Lubeznik Center for the Arts

#3: ALL PROCESS AND NO VISION

What's wrong: The chief executive is an internal, process-oriented person, with a strong ability to manage people and systems, but has no ability to paint a picture of future opportunity, either internally or externally, and no desire to move the organization on to its next incarnation.

Why this is a problem: As noted in the previous section, the most successful chief executives are able to excel at both internal and external functions. When a chief executive has no abilities in the visioning area, she is a mere manager of daily operations without attention to the future potential of the organization. An organization can become stagnant and lose effectiveness and competitiveness, as well as the support of key stakeholders who want to feel inspired by its vision and plans.

Case: As the chief executive of the Ordinary Day Fund, Jimmy VonVicker ran a really tight ship. Over the past five years, he had meticulously built a staff and processes to efficiently run the three programs he inherited. The organization always had a balanced budget, there was a respectable operating reserve, and the Fund enjoyed goodwill in the community. But there was no excitement!

Dannie Akers was one of the board members who were highly frustrated. There was so much need, yet anytime any of the board members suggested new programs or opportunities, VonVicker quickly shot them down. He just couldn't see any possibility of doing anything differently. His favorite saying was, "If it ain't broke, why fix it!"

What could have been done differently: Having someone who is good at running a well-oiled machine is not a bad problem to have. In fact, many boards would love to have this problem. However, the management needs of an organization change as circumstances change. Sticking with the status quo can become problematic when it contributes to lost opportunities, diminished competitiveness, and stagnation. Focusing on process only is not sufficient when there is an opportunity for the organization to move to the next level and take on a more compelling, ambitious, or exciting strategic direction.

What to do now: The board and staff can take stock of the present situation — and future challenges and opportunities — by conducting an organizational assessment combined with a strategic planning process. Among the questions that should guide this process are: Where are we? Where do we want to go? And what would success look like if we got there? Often, it is through this process that chief executives recognize that it is time for them to move on. At the very least, a thorough assessment can provide the necessary talking points for the board chair to have a conversation with the chief executive about present needs — and, if necessary, allow for an adieu that is warm, caring, supportive, and in everyone's best interest.

Conversation starter:

Akers: "Jimmy, I would like to engage the board in a different way and wanted to let you know that we are going to conduct a two-hour strategic thinking session at the next board meeting. We are going to break out into small groups and ask the question, 'If time, money, and other resources were no problem and we could wave a magic wand, what might we want to do to grow the Ordinary Day Fund?' We would like you and each of the members of the senior staff to be at one of those small groups, but to refrain from saying anything. We just want to get the juices flowing and see what might come up. I trust that you will support this effort. Who knows — we may all be surprised!"

THE PROBLEM OF PURPOSE

For many boards beset by problems of purpose, the costs of business as usual are enormous. The irrelevance, detachment, and underutilization of trustees lead to accountability failures; the boards most disengaged by inconsequential work are least able to sustain the vigilance needed for effective oversight. And problems of purpose can also impose costly dysfunctions on the organization. In search of meaningful work, frustrated trustees sometimes meddle in management. This exasperates executives and intensifies resentment among the staff, which often feels obliged, if only for purposes of political survival, to create the illusion that the board is both valuable and valued.

Source: *Governance as Leadership.* by Richard P. Chait, William R. Ryan, and Barbara E. Taylor (John Wiley & Sons, 2004).

#4: FAILING TO USE THE BOARD

What's wrong: The chief executive fails to use the time, talent, and treasure of the board for constructive purposes.

Why this is a problem: As the authors of *Governance as Leadership* have observed, board members provide necessary capital to organizations: intellectual, reputational, political, and social. An organization that is not using its board productively is missing out on opportunities. The board of directors and the chief executive are members of a team, with a shared responsibility to achieve the mission of the organization. When the team is not working together effectively, the organization's results and reputation can suffer.

Case: Lorna Nathanson was a frustrated and disengaged board member. When she was asked to become a member of the board of the Clowns of America Association, she knew it was because of her expertise in public relations and marketing. She was eager to help the organization.

However, she found out quickly that the board was a board in name only. Whenever she made a suggestion the chief executive, James Randall, would smile and say, "Yes, we've tried that" or "We thought about that but we can't really do it because...."

Nathanson had coffee with a few longtime board members after a recent meeting and found out that this was common practice. They were concerned — Randall always did everything himself, and sometimes not that well. He didn't know how to ask for help or to use the strength and the expertise of the board. Nathanson thought, "Well, this is going to be a waste of my time for the next three years."

What could have been done differently: Ideally, a chief executive has an opportunity to recognize each board member's areas of expertise and other strengths that could be used to aid an organization in accomplishing its goals. Why bring so many smart, ambitious, well-connected, dedicated people together and then not tap into that potential? Effective boards build their ranks strategically and bring individuals on board who are committed to using critically needed skills to expand the reach of the organization. But it is a two-step process — finding the right people and then being prepared to use them. Clarifying expectations for potential board members is also important. In the case above, Nathanson may have had unrealistic expectations about how she would be used as a board member.

What to do now: Working with the chief executive to ensure understanding of need, time, and resources is important. Potential questions for a discussion between Randall and the board chair might be

- How can we appropriately manage board member expectations in this regard?

- How can we ensure that the strengths of board members are fully utilized?

- How can we best manage the process of utilizing board members and best integrate their work within the context and time constraints of organizational need?

Here are some examples that a board and chief executive can do to recognize and increase board value in a way that best meets the needs of the organization:

- Conduct regular strategic thinking sessions about current and future issues.

- Have a "Rolodex" party to see who knows whom.

- Send out an S.O.S. asking for specific help on particular projects.

There is an opportunity for Nathanson to start the conversation with the board chair, perhaps suggesting that some time be dedicated at an upcoming board meeting to generatively discuss board engagement:

- How can we ensure that this board is more engaged, both individually and collectively?

- What would engagement look like?

- How would this further the mission?

From there, specific strategies can be developed that would help to shift the organizational culture and raise consciousness with the chief executive that the board will expect more in the future.

NECESSARY KNOWLEDGE
FINDING THE RIGHT MIX OF BOARD-CEO ENGAGEMENT

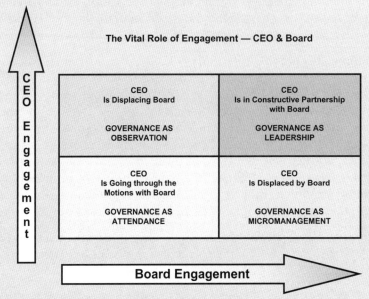

The Vital Role of Engagement — CEO & Board

CEO Engagement	CEO Is Displacing Board GOVERNANCE AS OBSERVATION	CEO Is in Constructive Partnership with Board GOVERNANCE AS LEADERSHIP
	CEO Is Going through the Motions with Board GOVERNANCE AS ATTENDANCE	CEO Is Displaced by Board GOVERNANCE AS MICROMANAGEMENT

Board Engagement

Source: Courtesy of Michael Daigneault, Senior Governance Consultant, BoardSource, modeled after Richard Chait, et al., *Governance as Leadership*.

#5: CREATING CLIQUES AND GROUP DIVISIONS

What's wrong: Whether intentionally or not, the chief executive makes decisions or acts in a way that creates subgroups within the larger group.

Why this is a problem: Cliques often work against each other to the detriment of the common goal. This behavior creates unrest in the organization and can wear down key stakeholders. It disrupts decision-making processes, causing lack of consensus and a tendency for each subgroup or faction to fight for its idea for the sake of winning, rather than listening with an open mind for the good of the cause. Ultimately, when board members expect board time to be consumed by incessant disagreement created by the chief executive, engagement and commitment begin to wane.

Case: Harry Long was hired as the chief executive of Tutors for Tomorrow's Leaders to be a change agent. Other organizations had sprung up recently that were providing similar programs and services to great community press and acclaim. The board wanted its new chief executive to undertake a strategic planning process as soon as he was acclimated to the organization. The board clearly sent Long that message in the interview process and again confirmed its message when he was hired.

The board chair, Sandra Williams, had looked forward to engaging the board and Long in a strategic planning process that would tackle some of the issues the board had already identified over the past year. However, a month went by and Long had failed to reach out to Williams. Long came from an organization where he had tremendous power and influence and a weak board. He did not seem to understand the expectations of the board in this regard. And, to make matters worse, Danny Morgan, the vice chair of the board, had arranged a lunch with Long the first week that he started and the two clicked. From that point on, they spent a good deal of time on the phone and exchanging e-mails — Long used Morgan as a sounding board for his ideas and Morgan was very impressed with Long's vision and grasp of the current realities.

At the next board meeting, Long presented a fully fleshed out proposal for strategic planning; it was clear that the proposed process had the advance review and strong support of Morgan. Williams felt marginalized and was concerned that the rest of the board had been as well. As time went on, these divisions strengthened. Long focused on cultivating Morgan as the next chair, as well as a small yet vocal and domineering group of board members as his "kitchen cabinet." Eventually, Long and this group turned the conversation away from the real issues and positioned the conflict as one in which Williams, as the board chair, was trying to micromanage Long. When Williams' term was up as chair, she and three other members resigned from the board.

What could have been done differently: During the hiring process, Williams could have sought clear agreement among the board members regarding the nature of the upcoming strategic planning process. The board also could have pushed for a formalized onboarding and orientation to ensure a shared understanding between Williams and Long. In hindsight, Morgan probably should not have arranged the private lunch with Long, or discussed "offline" ideas about the strategic planning process. And once it became clear that there was a problem, Williams could have called the board into executive session (without Long) to discuss the board's behavior and find an opportunity to come to consensus and present a united front to the chief executive.

What to do now: If this happened once, it may happen again. A practice of allowing the chief executive to enjoy "special relationships" with one or more board members — i.e., relationships in which organizational discussions, recommendations, and decisions are fleshed out by the few — can lead to a chief executive who may assert too much control or who may manipulate one or more board members against others to influence a particular outcome. Someone will need to step up and suggest that the board have governance training or conduct a self-assessment to ensure that all board members have an awareness of appropriate board behavior.

NECESSARY KNOWLEDGE
MAKING USE OF EXECUTIVE SESSIONS: WHEN IS AN EXECUTIVE SESSION NECESSARY?

The following circumstances may demand confidentiality, candid exchange of opinions, protection of individual rights, or need to improve board performance:

- investigation of alleged improper conduct by a board member

- discussion of financial issues with an auditor

- preparation for a case with a lawyer

- exploration of planning for major endeavors, such as mergers or real estate deals

- discussion of the board's approach to a scandal or negative publicity

- handling of personnel issues, such as chief executive compensation, performance evaluation, or disciplinary issues

- handling of any other matters where confidentiality has been requested or is otherwise prudent

- peer-to-peer discussions about board operations

There are also clear rules when an executive session is not in order. Boards should not revert to executive sessions for any of the following reasons: to avoid discussing tough issues in the open; to dodge responsibility; to restrict any board member's access to information by excluding him or her from a meeting; to purposefully create a secret society atmosphere and air of suspicion. The purpose of the session must be clear ahead of time and as soon as the issue has been handled, a regular meeting should proceed. The chair is responsible for calling these sessions and using them appropriately, but any board member may request one. Bylaws or board policies determine how to proceed.

Chief executives sometimes feel threatened by closed meetings from which they are excluded. For example: A chief executive was distressed when she realized that the board was suddenly meeting alone and barred her, specifically, from the room. Afterwards it became clear that the board wanted to plan the details for a special anniversary in her honor. To ease unnecessary worries, the board must communicate with the chief executive following the session and inform him or her of possible conclusions or recommendations that surfaced during the meeting. If the board holds these meetings on a regular basis — for instance, before or after each board meeting — suspicions can be dispelled. Trust and regular open communication will alleviate apprehension.

Source: *Meeting, and Exceeding Expectations* by Outi Flynn (BoardSource, 2009).

#6: CRITICIZING THE ORGANIZATION IN PUBLIC

What's wrong: The chief executive makes critical or disparaging comments about the board, the organization, or another affiliated person in a public forum.

Why this is a problem: If the chief executive criticizes the organization and its people in a public setting, he or she can single-handedly compromise the organization's reputation and public goodwill, while possibly sharing confidential information about its operations.

Case: It was clear from the start that Phoebe Lancaster may not have been the right person for the job. The committee did all the right things — had a strong process, asked all the right questions, did the reference checks, and even used a consultant. But soon after Lancaster was hired, it was as though she was a different person from the one they had interviewed. Several board members expressed a sense of uneasiness about her. She was not a very inviting person.

Lancaster had several missteps in her first six months. She did not follow board-stated policy in an incident regarding a staff member. She was an hour late to a cultivation event and behaved as if she was just another guest instead of a key organizational representative who was there to meet and greet important people from the community. At subsequent fundraising events, she and the staff had to be coerced to help. Lancaster never helped to set up or clean up, always arrived late, and most distressingly, simply did not mingle. The board felt this was a missed opportunity at the very least. And then there were the inadequate reports to the board. It was clear that the budget was a mess, but because the board wasn't getting any regular financial reporting, it had no idea how to track where the organization stood.

More important, board members began to hear things in the community about the organization. In one instance, Lancaster was having dinner at one of the power restaurants in town and talking to her dinner companions disparagingly about her job and the organization. "All I can say is that this organization is really not what I signed up for," she said. "It is small and parochial. Get this: We recently ran out of money and had to get emergency funding just to make payroll. Imagine, I can't even be sure of my next paycheck!" She didn't realize a reporter for the local newspaper and a good friend of the board chair overheard her conversation.

What could have been done differently: It appears that this board did everything it could in the interview process to hire the right person for the job. Unfortunately, hiring is not an exact science and even the best and most diligent process does not always yield the right fit. As issues unfolded, the board had an opportunity to begin documenting them in an objective and factual manner in case there was a need to justify a termination.

What to do now: If and when the reporter informs the board chair of what she heard, the board chair should immediately have a candid conversation with the chief executive. Having specific factual information — place, date, time, and who heard what — is the only way that this conversation can have legitimacy. Speaking poorly of the organization in public, regardless of whether or not confidential information is publicized, is unacceptable behavior and the chief executive should be held accountable. The fallout of the negative publicity could make this situation even worse for the organization.

Conversation Starter:

Board chair: "Phoebe, something's come to my attention and it's a little embarrassing. At around 8 p.m. on March 17, you were overheard at The Place Restaurant talking about our organization, our board, and some of our financial issues. Unfortunately, someone heard you say some very critical things about the organization and that you had concerns about our activities and viability.

"I bring this up for two reasons. The first is that I'm surprised that I have to remind you that we have to be careful about what we say when we are in public and to whom. As you know, we live in a very small community. Second, this information indicates to me and the board that you are not happy in your job. It would have been better if you had shared your concerns with me. If there is something we can do to improve the situation for everyone, perhaps we can come to those conclusions together. Now, is there anything you would like to share with me before we decide together what we need to do?"

NECESSARY KNOWLEDGE

Like many large public organizations, the McDonald's Corporation often finds itself faced with a situation or circumstance that could easily develop into a public relations nightmare due to a lack of complete information on the part of the public. When discussing and scenario planning these situations, Robert Langert, vice president of Corporate Citizenship and Issues Management, and his team always try to "stay on the left side of the curve." The opportunity for an organization to manage public perception is well before a triggering event. Otherwise it might snowball into an escalated or incorrect version of the circumstances. A triggering event can be avoided by actively determining who needs to know what and quickly sharing this information in the best way possible. The graph below illustrates their process.

SOCIAL RESPONSIBILITY ISSUES: ANTICIPATING, MONITORING AND ACTING

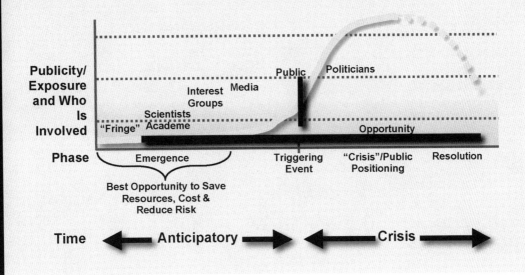

SECTION 2
INCOMPETENCE

Incompetence can be defined in a variety of ways, such as an inability to perform, or ineptitude. In the case of an incompetent chief executive it can be blatant or be shaded with subtleties that make taking action challenging. The two cases presented in this section demonstrate these two extremes and provide some food for thought as to possible next steps.

#7: IMPULSIVITY OR FINANCIAL RECKLESSNESS

What's wrong: The chief executive undertakes costly new initiatives without thinking them through, or makes poor decisions that negatively affect the organization.

Why this is a problem: Reckless or negligent behavior with regard to an organization's finances (e.g., taking on a new initiative without proper vetting of full consideration of organizational capacity and goals) can put the organization's reputation or financial stability at risk. A pattern of poor decisions is an indication that the chief executive is not using sound reasoning or does not have a strong foundation of knowledge and information on which to base actions.

Case: When Amelia Erickson was hired as chief executive of Columbia County's Friendship House, the board and staff were eager to hear her fresh take on the challenges and opportunities facing the organization. She was an accomplished advocate with a high profile and a solid reputation, but this was her first chief executive position, and she did not have a solid understanding of finances or operations. She often made decisions impulsively. Her first idea: building one facility to provide services to the homeless in the county, rather than relying on local places of worship to open their doors as temporary overnight shelters with Friendship House providing trained volunteers, food, and other supplies, as the organization had always done.

Erickson kept pushing her vision of a stand-alone facility owned and operated by Friendship House, and eventually the board agreed to build the new building. Within a year after the facility opened, however, Erickson, aware that the organization was running into money trouble, moved to another job without sharing her concerns with the board. When Daniel Jones started as the new chief executive, it didn't take him long to understand that Friendship House was bleeding and that it would have to cut services for its homeless clients just to survive.

What could have been done differently: Often, boards select chief executives who have high visibility or a strong industry reputation. The hope is that this validates the organization in the eyes of the general public and key stakeholders. However, a board would be negating its duty of care, particularly with respect to financial oversight, if it did not ensure that the chief executive also has a strong financial background or an understanding of organizational finance and stewardship.

A board has an opportunity as well as an obligation to set expectations for sound financial management of an organization. One way it can ensure this is to insist that the chief executive work with a chief financial officer. In addition to ensuring that policies are followed, internal controls are in place, and the financial infrastructure is monitored, chief financial officers may recognize early financial weaknesses in the form of undisciplined expenditures, or point out opportunities to generate new revenue streams. A strong CFO, along with a strong board finance committee with clearly defined policies and reporting requirements, will help to ensure organizational sustainability and prevent shoddy decision making.

Boards can get swept away by the excitement and enthusiasm that comes with change. In their desire to support the chief executive they hired, board members neglected some crucial steps that would have informed their decision-making process. Starting with strategic planning or an organizational capacity audit before making such a monumental decision might have helped. A comprehensive feasibility study regarding the new facility — including an understanding of the long-term operational costs — would have provided critical information to the original decision-making process.

What to do now: Now is a time for reflection and action — reflection on what went wrong and action to ensure that it does not happen again. The board and the new chief executive should consider changes in the composition of the board to ensure that it has the right talent mix to manage a turnaround, including a strong fundraising capacity to ensure that it has the resources to deliver needed services. The board also should consider working toward creating an endowment to ensure future sustainability, while creating board processes that ensure fuller deliberation of challenges and opportunities confronting the organization.

GET THE BEST FROM YOUR CHIEF EXECUTIVE

It's important to have very clear roles for the chief executive and the board, a good working relationship between board chair and chief, a shared proud sense of and belief in the mission, and a well-grounded sense of humor.

Jacqueline Gilbert
Board Member and Co-Chair, Board Development Practice
Executive Service Corps of Chicago

#8: RESISTING NEW OPPORTUNITIES

What's wrong: The chief executive is closed-minded to something new or different and stands in the way of necessary growth and change.

Why this is a problem: As an organization grows and adapts to external changes, the work and structure of the board and staff also needs to change in order to keep the organization successful and relevant in its community. When a chief executive gets in the way of necessary change, opportunities are lost and the organization could be at risk for stagnation.

Case: Jack Murphy was the chair of the Caldwell Music Center. Its longtime chief executive, Julie Atkins, had served the organization well until this past year. The trouble started when the Center received notice of the bequest of a building — a stunning mansion that was too good to be true. When it was announced at a board meeting, everyone bubbled with excitement and started brainstorming about the renovations the building would need for adaptation to the Center's use.

The morning after the meeting, Murphy got a call from the chief executive. Atkins told him that she didn't think the Center should try to renovate the building. Rather, she proposed that it be sold and the proceeds put into an endowment for future operations. Atkins shared that she had gone through a capital campaign before and it had ruined that organization.

At the next board meeting, Atkins was asked to share her thoughts. Previously, the board blindly listened to and followed her recommendations, but in this case, the reaction was different. Board members could not reconcile Atkins's proposal with her many previous statements about the need to find a more permanent space. They knew this was an exceptional opportunity and were convinced that they could raise the money needed. The discussion took up the entire meeting.

The board created a task force to conduct member interviews and vet the pros and the cons of a capital campaign, and Atkins was asked to be present. She failed to attend any of the meetings. The task force ultimately recommended that the Center keep the building and mount a capital campaign to raise funds for the renovations. At the meeting where the board discussed and accepted the recommendation, Atkins threw up her hands and stormed out.

From then on, Atkins refused to have any role in the process. She opposed meeting with the architect to provide ideas about what might be needed to support current programming. She stalled on sharing the membership or donor lists with board members who were eager to begin to make asks. But, perhaps most egregiously, she actively fought the process by contacting stakeholders to "share her deep concerns." Atkins was at total odds with the board and actively tried to cause dissension.

The board's next difficult discussion was about whether or not the Center could continue to have a chief executive who was in active opposition to the direction agreed upon by the board. It was a poisonous atmosphere. The board consulted attorneys and others and was advised on how to proceed. At the scheduled board meeting with Atkins to share concerns and expectations, she stood up, threw the keys at a board member, said "I quit" and left.

What could have been done differently: It is not clear if anything could have been done differently. It may have been more of a case of the chief executive's discomfort and anger that the board didn't follow her recommendation rather than of her being against the building acquisition and capital campaign. Or perhaps she had a fear of failure. In that case, more diligence on the part of the board to ascertain the source of her strong opposition and to try to bring her around may have helped.

What to do now: The board has an opportunity to talk through what the organization needs in terms of leadership and to develop a strong process for the recruitment, vetting, and onboarding of the next chief executive.

SECTION 3

INSUBORDINATION

What often appears to be an insubordinate chief executive is usually the failure of a chief executive to understand the scope and limits of his power, authority, and accountability. Failing to follow through; undermining the board chair; withholding information; acting without authority; missing deadlines; or deviating from policy, mission, or budget are addressed in this section.

#9: NO FOLLOW-THROUGH ON PROMISES TO THE BOARD

What's wrong: The chief executive either promises or is assigned to undertake a certain course of action and then fails to do so.

Why this is a problem: When a chief executive doesn't follow through on her promises to the board, or doesn't carry out assigned tasks, this can lead to an erosion of trust at best and threaten mission fulfillment at worst.

Case: The Popkin Care Center provided a small outreach office with supplies and access to resources for people dealing with recovery from substance abuse. Its new chief executive, Marian Henderson, was the only employee and she was not effective in her job. As an affiliate program of a statewide organization, there were certain reports and activities that were required. It appeared to the board that Henderson did just enough to keep the main office satisfied, but when the board requested a set of standard reports on a monthly basis, Henderson didn't comply. Sometimes the board would get a report out of the blue, but often she came to meetings unprepared. Ultimately, the organization was being run by the volunteer board. Henderson finally resigned after a year and a half and the board was so burned by the experience that it has asked the state organization for permission to not have an employee.

What could have been done differently: Sometimes chief executives simply don't do what they agreed to do. It may be an innocent oversight, in which case a simple reminder is required, or it may be because the chief executive doesn't agree with the reason for the action in the first place. Clarifying expectations in advance is the best way to prevent this kind of problem from occurring.

What to do now: Working without a chief executive may seem appealing in the short term, but having the volunteer board members run the organization may cause burnout. Instead of forgoing a chief executive completely, the board could work to clarify its expectations for prospective employees, work on strengthening its search and hiring practices, and develop a strong mechanism for oversight. Engaging the help of the parent organization may also prove useful.

#10: UNDERMINING THE BOARD CHAIR

What's wrong: The chief executive does not honor the volunteer commitment or the legal designation of the individual serving in the board chair role.

Why this is a problem: Maintaining a high-quality relationship between the board chair and the chief executive requires a significant level of commitment, maturity, and understanding from both people. This relationship can become dysfunctional because of misunderstandings, failure to clarify roles and expectations, or interpersonal conflicts. A dysfunctional relationship, in turn, can threaten the organization's progress.

Case: Maddy Johnson had been on the board of the Purposeful Charter School for 10 years and had now become the board chair. It was clear soon after she took on that role that the chief executive, Joel Taylor, wanted a board chair in name only. It turned out that he had been selecting the board chair for years. Johnson guessed that Taylor regretted selecting her. It actually came as a shock to him that she had ideas about how the board should work. Historically, this board let Taylor lead them. Johnson now realized that there has really never been any real reporting, no transparency, and the board had no real idea or understanding of how things work.

As time went on, Taylor was often argumentative with Johnson and later she found out that he was the same way with former board chairs that asked questions or put forth ideas regarding any change in board/organizational culture.

Johnson said, "I spent countless hours in meetings with Joel to try to flush out our differences and figure out ways to effectively work together. But I finally concluded that he didn't want to have a peer relationship with a board chair. He may have agreed in front of me, but behind the scenes, he was complaining to other board members. He wanted to control the board. He made my life miserable and threatened to quit and take the staff 'with him' unless I resigned. Joel was not truthful with the rest of the board about what happened between us — I had started out by asking legitimate questions in an effort to understand and suggested that we may want to have greater transparency with the board and the public. He implied that I was trying to micromanage and do his job. He badmouthed me to the rest of the board. I have since resigned. I feel I was forced to. Many of these board members were my friends, some of whom I knew for 15 years or more. Now, it is very awkward seeing them around town. It has really divided the community and not served the organization well."

What could have been done differently: It appears that the board of this organization failed to understand its governance responsibility and instead let the chief executive run the board. Without a solid understanding on both sides of the respective roles of the board and the chief executive, it is easy for one or the other to dominate. Boards have a responsibility to be more diligent about their oversight with a chief executive.

An alternate strategy for the board chair may have been to begin to introduce questions about certain issues at full board meetings in order to build board understanding. Using an external consultant may also have assisted in this process. To the extent that these actions lead to the departure of board members or the chief executive (because they cannot adapt to the power shift), then so be it. The organization's future success depends on clarity about roles and responsibilities, and on a strong working relationship between the board and chief executive.

The board chair also could have tried to explain the problem to the rest of the board before trying to address the concerns with the chief executive. Conducting a chief executive assessment also may have fleshed out the problems in a more constructive manner. Either of these may have prevented the situation from turning personal.

What to do now: The board chair has attempted to resolve the relationship challenges in constructive ways. The fact that the full board supported the chief executive rather than the board chair illustrates the dynamics of this particular organization and the presence of a controlling chief executive. Until other board members recognize the situation for what it is and understand and embrace their fiduciary responsibilities more deeply, it is unlikely that this organization will change. Perhaps the next board chair will raise similar concerns and board members will start to see patterns, or perhaps the chief executive will finally move on. But until then, the organization will operate from an essentially compromised position, with a board unwilling to step up to its rightful governance role.

#11: NOT KEEPING THE BOARD INFORMED

What's wrong: The chief executive does not provide regular information to the board, or presents the information in a way that does not allow the board to monitor progress.

Why this is a problem: Lack of information and deficiencies in reporting can erode board trust in the chief executive. In addition, it can lead to board member disengagement or loss of morale, while preventing the board from fulfilling its fiduciary responsibility.

Case: Kara Lincoln was a very bright young chief executive. Many people thought she had great promise, and the board at the Cardinal Botanical Garden felt that it was very lucky to have hired her. However, within the first few months, it became clear that she moved pretty fast. The regular updates and reports that the board had been used to from the previous chief executive were just not forthcoming. In addition, Lincoln only used e-mail, so when the reports did come, not all board members had ready access to them.

What could have been done differently: During onboarding, the board had an opportunity to share its expectations regarding the reporting of information with Lincoln. Chief executives can't read minds. On the other side, an incoming chief executive has an opportunity and responsibility to ask about board member expectations. The chief executive should sound out the board on the question of reporting — how often and in what formats does it want to hear from her?

What to do now: It is important for the board and the chief executive to take time to discuss reporting and communications. This may require some stretching on both sides. The chief executive, for example, may need to devote more time to providing the board with regular updates, and to doing so in a variety of formats (i.e., not just e-mail). Board members, on the other hand, may need to accept that they can't be offline as much as they used to if they want to stay engaged in the work of the organization.

Discussions between the chief executive and the board can begin with some of the following questions:

- *What information to share:* What information do board members really need to fulfill their oversight role? Is the information provided critical to monitoring against stated goals, or is it just interesting show and tell? Can the organization use dashboard reporting effectively?

- *How to share it:* How should information be shared? Should the chief executive send out e-mails with .pdf attachments? Should she provide hard-copy mailings? Should board members be asked to come to the office to pick up a packet on an established basis? Should reporting happen only at committee and full board meetings? Should the organization establish an online board portal where all information can be posted on a regular basis and for reference and archiving purposes?

- *When to share it:* When do board members need this information? Should the board and chief executive designate actual dates for reporting so everyone knows what to expect, and when?

#12: ACTING WITHOUT AUTHORITY

What's wrong: The chief executive, believing that the board only exists to rubber stamp his decisions, insists on actions or strategies without seeking board discussion and consensus.

Why this is a problem: This behavior can be irritating and demotivating and in many cases can cost the organization time and money by taking programs or decisions in the wrong direction.

Case: New board member Patricia Coswell quickly discovered that the board of Give a Kid a Computer had hired a chief executive with a very imperialistic view of what it means to be a chief executive. It was clear from his communications to the board that he believed that boards should approve his vision and actions without question. Coswell came to believe that their new chief executive had a previous experience like that and assumed that this board would be the same.

The turning point came when the chief executive hired an audit firm without consulting the board. He had used this audit firm at his previous place of employment and thought that they had done a great job. Many of the board members knew of this firm and there wasn't really an objection to them or their work. However, for several of the board members, there was an objection to the process and, as some put it, "…the chief executive's dictatorial decree that there shouldn't be any discussion about a decision that he had already made." When Coswell and a couple of other board members challenged that assumption, suggesting better practices and insisting that certain decisions needed to be vetted or made by the board, the chief executive became incensed.

What could have been done differently: During the search process, the search committee could have explored more deeply the management style of the chief executive and his relationship with his previous board(s). Asking open-ended questions about how the chief executive interacted with the board and the nature of that board's process may have been very enlightening. Once hired, this board could have been more diligent in sharing its expectations with the chief executive about this issue, particularly in light of the Sarbanes-Oxley Act and its implications for nonprofit organizations (see the 2006 joint publication by BoardSource and Independent Sector titled *The Sarbanes-Oxley Act and Implications for Nonprofit Organizations*).

What to do now: Providing the chief executive with constructive feedback is required here. Coming from a place of respect, discuss the expectations of this board with regard to communications and etiquette, the desired quality of the chief-executive relationship, and a review of any executive limitations policies would provide an opportunity to clear the air and foster a fresh start.

GET THE BEST FROM YOUR CHIEF EXECUTIVE

This is the single most important advice I can offer, and it has left me with 30 years of great chair/CEO relationships. "I promise I will never surprise you in front of the board or in public and you will never surprise me…deal?" (Shake on it.)

Eliot Pfanstiehl
President/CEO
Strathmore Hall Foundation, Inc.

#13: MISSING ESTABLISHED GOALS

What's wrong: The chief executive misses established goals or benchmarks agreed to by the board as a way to track organizational outcomes.

Why this is a problem: In order to achieve the organization's mission, the board and chief executive must work together to establish realistic benchmarks and goals that are tied to a clear timeline. Missing these benchmarks or goals suggests a problem — either hopes are too high or execution toward goals is lacking. Whatever the case, the board has an obligation to ascertain what's wrong.

Case: Johnny Dover was chair of a regional church board made up of member representatives from several churches. In his first few months in the position, he worked with the board to produce a meaningful and transparent goal-setting process and monitoring mechanism for the coming year. Now the challenge was to set up a process to monitor progress toward those goals. Dover was not sure of the next steps, and the chief executive didn't seem to want to be a part of the process at all. She was only reluctantly involved in the goal-setting process in the first place — and Dover knew that his predecessor as chair had a similar problem with her. The board had set several benchmarks that would indicate achievement toward organizational goals, and not only did the chief executive regularly miss them, but the board never received an adequate explanation as to why this happened.

What could have been done differently: In this case, it appears that not enough work was done to get the chief executive's buy-in to the goal-setting process. Getting buy-in is about convincing others that it is in their interest to participate; buy-in helps ensure that you have another party's understanding, commitment, and action to support goals. Especially in matters of setting and working toward organizational goals, boards should know that buy-in from the chief executive is essential. Results can't be dictated from on high. People will resist and may even try to prevent work toward goals that they feel have been imposed by others. Involving all key stakeholders in this work as part of the goal-setting process is what successful teams do.

What to do now: One of the best ways to achieve buy-in is to have the entire team use stories or "scenario planning" to create a picture of a positive future for the organization. A powerful question to ask is, "If we did that, what would success look like?"

In addition, those involved need to know what's in it for them. Listen to what they have to say and work together to create possible goals from everyone's perspective. While goals should usually be somewhat of a stretch, they do need to be realistic and doable. The chief executive has the critical vantage point of knowing the organizational resources available to hit the marks on the path along the way to goal achievement — what can be done, by whom, and by what time.

If you do the goal-setting work right, with genuine engagement of the chief executive and others, establishing the monitoring mechanism should be a relatively easy task.

If the chief executive continues to resist involvement, the board chair has an obligation to directly address the issue in order to achieve understanding of the reluctance and gain a commitment to a more positive course of action. Failing that, bringing in an outside consultant to try to mediate the issue may be helpful. Finally, stubborn resistance for no apparent reason may need to be documented in the chief executive's personnel file for consideration on or before the next performance review. Direct behavior contrary to a board's directive may require immediate personnel action.

GET THE BEST FROM YOUR CHIEF EXECUTIVE

As a CEO, I am most productive when my board president trusts me to do my job, gives wise advice, supports me, and accepts that I'm human and will make mistakes.

Esther Newman
Founder & Executive Director
Leadership Montgomery (MD)

#14: DEVIATING FROM POLICY

What's wrong: The chief executive does not comply with agreed-upon organizational policy.

Why this is a problem: Deviation from policy undermines board trust in the chief executive. At worst, it can compromise the organization's reputation and/or its ability to achieve its mission.

Case: A major commercial development was announced for Egret Island. As the long-time chief executive of Save the American Egret Now, Linda Jones wanted to act ASAP to try and stop the development. She contracted with a new public relations firm in town that offered to produce a public service announcement quickly and at a very reasonable cost. Despite board-approved policy requiring three bids for any contract of this size, Jones felt confident the board would agree to work with the new firm because of the timing and the cost. Jones thought, "Because of the nature of this specific situation, it's better for me to beg forgiveness later than to lose time by asking permission now."

What could have been done differently: In general, it is not advisable for a chief executive to ignore policy, particularly if the policy has been crafted with care and forethought by a governing board for the protection of an organization. Jones should have informed the board chair of her intended actions and gotten approval for going with the solo bid. Alternatively, she should have followed the policy of soliciting three bids, even if it would take extra time.

What to do now: If the board trusts Jones's judgment, it can consider establishing an exception policy for cases like this. Such a policy would allow the chief executive to take action if he or she feels that it is critical to do so without following policy or seeking board approval for deviating from policy, perhaps with the concurrence of the board chair or the executive committee or a minimum number of board members consulted. The exception policy would need to be carefully considered and crafted and the circumstances under which it would be employed made clear. Any decision taken under the described circumstances would need a formalized and documented ratification of the chief executive's action in subsequent board minutes.

Of course, not all instances of a chief executive deviating from policy are alike. For example, if a chief executive deviates from policy because he or she does not quite understand it, coaching from the board is required. If a chief executive deviates from policy because he or she does not agree with the policy, the board chair and the chief executive need to have a candid conversation. The board chair must remind the chief executive of his or her obligation to comply with policy regardless of personal opinion. The conversation also provides an opportunity to review the policy. Sometimes policies become outdated or are not easy to comply with in the face of competing priorities. If the chief executive can make a good evidentiary case for a policy change, then the board has an obligation to consider it.

If a chief executive deviates from policy because he or she feels superior to the board (i.e., does not feel that he or she needs to follow policies), the situation is obviously one requiring formal personnel action. The board should not support or condone repeated behavior in this regard.

Regardless of the situation and the motivation, in all of the above, the board chair should document the action and resulting conversation in the chief executive's personnel file just in case.

#15: DEVIATING FROM THE MISSION

What's wrong: The board or chief executive decides to undertake initiatives or activities that are not directly related to the stated mission of the organization.

Why this is a problem: If a board or a chief executive deviates from the stated mission, programs and activities central to the mission can be compromised and in some cases the organization's nonprofit status can be at risk.

Case: When the board of Friends of the Johnson Center needed to replace a long-term founding chief executive, they hired a high-profile and seemingly competent person with great credentials. Judy Stevens had a reputation for coming in and helping organizations operate at peak efficiency. But in her new position, it seemed she was making a lot of decisions that didn't align with the organization's mission. Stevens added programs that many board members didn't feel were a good fit for the organization, and she signed a five-year lease for new headquarters at a significantly higher cost. Stevens thought she had the right to do these things, and the organization's policies were in her favor — largely because the organization had never seen the need to review their policies before. The previous chief executive didn't operate in this way. The executive committee felt that Stevens was overstepping her bounds.

What could have been done differently: Before hiring a new executive, the board should have reviewed its policies and strategic plan to ensure that everyone on the board had the same understanding of priority. With the advent of a new chief executive, the board should tighten up its policies and control mechanisms as necessary. During the interviewing process, the board should share plans and policies with all candidates and set expectations about board-driven priorities.

What to do now: Working closely with the chief executive, the board should launch a review of organizational policies to see where they can be tightened and clarified. The dialogue should be based on an acknowledgment by the board that the organization's policies may not have been as tight as they could have been — and that Stevens was, for the most part, merely trying to move the organization forward. If the chief executive is savvy, she may already be aware that moving too quickly may have undermined confidence in her leadership, and that the board's concerns are not personal. The chief executive can actively help the board shape policies that will allow her to move forward with their full support.

GET THE BEST FROM YOUR CHIEF EXECUTIVE

A real sense of accomplishment and satisfaction for a chief executive officer is "winning a personal challenge." A good CEO is not content with a run-of-the-mill operation, but wants to reach that next level, thus the challenge.

Mike Cherry
CEO
Consumer Credit Counseling Springfield, Missouri

#16: FAILING TO STICK TO A BUDGET

What's wrong: The chief executive overspends an approved operational budget, and/or falls short of achieving income goals for the organization.

Why this is a problem: While an organization can survive some level of deficit spending, going substantially over budget or failing to bring in income as projected can pose a threat to organizational finances and sustainability, particularly if this happens year after year.

Case: Alex Babcock was the artistic director of Ballet of America. Everyone acknowledged that he was brilliant — each presentation was a masterwork. Before Sandy Cullison was brought in as the new treasurer of the board, she had been given a heads-up by her predecessor that Babcock did not always stay within the budget. Keith Jacobs was the long-time CFO, but he basically did whatever the artistic director wanted, especially since the board never challenged Babcock in the past.

Sure enough, three weeks before the next production, Cullison saw on a report that Babcock had ordered four new follow spotlights at a cost of $7,950 each. Technically, this was a capital expense and the organization had already spent down its capital budget for the year. Babcock was charging it to the production line for this show — which would mean that this line would be overspent by more than $20,000. "How are we going to manage this on top of the $15,000 deficit from last year?" Cullison wondered.

What could have been done differently: Were four new follow spots critical to this production? From an artistic perspective, they may well have been. However, going into deficit year after year will ultimately prevent the ballet from carrying out its artistic mission over the long term — they may just go out of business. In this case, once a pattern of overspending emerged, the board should have made it absolutely clear to the artistic director and senior staff that they need to honor the fiscal constraints they agreed to.

What to do now: Board and staff need to engage in candid conversations about organizational sustainability and the responsibility of fiscal discipline, especially in light of deficits carrying over from prior years. There is a give-and-take to running an artistic organization — a natural tension between art and business. But if everyone understands that one cannot survive without the other, the organization is already halfway toward the goal of year-to-year viability.

SECTION 4
ILLEGAL OR UNETHICAL BEHAVIOR

The illegal or unethical activity of a chief executive in fulfilling his or her responsibilities is rare; but, when it does occur, it can have a catastrophic effect on the organization. Illegal or unethical activities can happen for a variety of reasons in many different contexts or settings and this section addresses just some of those possibilities. Regardless of the offense, the board, as the keeper of the public trust, is still liable for the entire organization and must take action to correct these behaviors. In addition to having clear policies and safeguards, a prudent board should always be forthcoming with legal information. Fighting criminal activity is bad enough. Battling charges of a board cover-up can be disastrous. Also, it is imperative — as taxing as it might be — to report any fraudulent activity to appropriate officials. Otherwise this individual might go to another organization and repeat the same offense.

#17: LYING

What's wrong: The chief executive makes blatantly false statements or purposefully misleads members of the board.

Why this is a problem: Dishonesty creates lack of trust that is rarely possible to reverse. Lying on the part of the chief executive also can compromise the integrity of the organization to the extent that the board has misleading or bogus information about critical operational issues.

Case: The new chief executive of the Lawyers Legal Aid Initiative, Nate Jefferson, was a hard person to work for. He gave 150 percent and expected others to do so the same. The trouble was, Nate was not organized. He did everything at the last minute, always in crisis mode. Jack Thompson, the chief financial officer, had been with the organization for about seven years. He knew that he did a good job and that the board, in particular, had appreciated his dedication and efforts. But after 15 months with Jefferson, Thompson just couldn't take the frenetic pace anymore. As much as Thompson hated to leave, he finally found another job and wrote his resignation letter. When Thompson met with Jefferson to tell him the news, it was as though Thompson had told Jefferson he was going to shoot him. Jefferson was furious and ordered Thompson out of the office and off the premises. Thompson couldn't believe it.

The next day, Jefferson called the board chair, Darren Arnold, and told him that Thompson had been caught "cooking the books" and that he had to let him go. Arnold was flabbergasted. This was not the Thompson he knew. He was quite upset and after hanging up with Jefferson, called several other board members to say they had an unfortunate personnel problem that would probably require legal action against Thompson. At the next board meeting a week later, Arnold opened the discussion with a recap, telling the board that Thompson had been caught by Jefferson in some questionable financial activities and that Jefferson had to fire Thompson. However, when Arnold asked Jefferson to give a report, he expressed some outrage and said that he never told Arnold any such thing. Everyone was very confused and concerned. Darren finally felt compelled to track Thompson down and ask him what had happened. Thompson told Arnold the facts and sent him a copy of his resignation letter. It was clear that Jefferson had lied.

What could have been done differently: Honesty is essential in any professional situation, especially when the success of an entire organization is at stake. Proper orientation or coaching/training could not have prevented this situation from happening — one cannot claim ignorance or a lack of awareness of the need to be honest.

What to do now: Employees who lie to their superiors or chief executives who lie to their boards about critical organizational issues must be let go. The board also has an obligation to ensure that the organization has well-crafted human resources policies that include removal for dishonest behavior. In addition, the board should make sure that the organization's hiring policies include sufficient reference checks and other actions that can help ensure that new hires have a solid reputation among previous employers.

GET THE BEST FROM YOUR CHIEF EXECUTIVE

Ensure he or she knows the goals of the organization, use metrics to track performance toward those goals, and take quick action if the goals are not being achieved. Holding the CEO accountable is essential.

Joyce Henderson, Ed.D.
Professor of Business and Management
University of Maryland University College

#18: SEEKING OR RECEIVING INAPPROPRIATE FINANCIAL RETURN FROM OUTSIDE AFFILIATIONS

What's wrong: The chief executive uses his or her affiliation with the organization to gain financial benefits.

Why this is a problem: Private inurement is illegal behavior. If this behavior becomes public, the organization will face a scandal and lose credibility.

Case: Tom Butler was the longtime chief executive of a real estate association. Every year, the largest mortgage lending company in the county would invite him to speak at the annual meeting. Butler felt that doing this was part of his job — although in the past few years, he really wished that he didn't have to do it. He was missing time with his family and it was a predictable event with not very good food.

One year, the mortgage lending company was having some public relations issues and decided that it needed to do things differently. The firm asked Butler if he would provide them with a list of contact information for the top 50 real estate agents in the county so they could be invited to a special pre-meeting dinner. In exchange, they offered to pay Butler a $5,000 honorarium for speaking at the dinner.

Butler was thrilled! Deep down he knew that the payment was really for the list, but this seemed like a good way to make everyone happy. "Actually," he thought, "I really deserve this. I have been speaking at this dinner for the past 15 years. When you think about it this way, that's really less than $350 per year that I probably should have been paid!"

What could have been done differently: Chief executives often are asked to speak at events. This is part of their job. Many organizations have a clear policy regarding honoraria earned — i.e., any honoraria or fees earned in a staff member's capacity as an organization's employee must be paid to or turned over to the organization. In this case, Butler should have notified the organization of the honorarium offer and should have been aware of a potential problem regarding the sale of the membership list.

What to do now: This is a situation that may never come to a board's attention. The organization, however, would be wise to develop a policy to help guide an employee into making the right decision. If the payment does come to light, the board must deal with it directly. To protect the organization's integrity, the money should either be turned over to the organization or returned. Since this honorarium payment had a hidden quid pro quo, returning the money to the company is probably the wiser thing to do. In addition, the board may wish to have a conversation with the company about the ethical nature of the original request and payment and may decide to make public the interaction with its members. Regarding Butler's lapse in judgment, the board has an opportunity to determine whether this was a one-time situation or a pattern of behavior. Obviously, the consequences of the latter should be addressed formally and documented accordingly in case there is a personnel action in the future.

#19: ENGAGING IN ILLEGAL ACTIVITY

What's wrong: The chief executive does something that is illegal.

Why this is a problem: Illegal acts can be nothing less than devastating to nonprofits, since they tarnish the organization's all-important reputation.

Case: The Otherly Abled Agency was a nonprofit that served individuals with developmental disabilities. Bryan Nichols was its long-time chief executive. Bryan, a staff person, and a friend from the community decided to start a for-profit organization that would employ the clients of the agency. After a year, one of the other staff members went to one of the organization's major funders and reported that Nichols was siphoning money off the nonprofit into the for-profit. The police were called and a high-profile investigation was launched. The board of directors fired Nichols.

What could have been done differently: More effective fiscal oversight may have brought this activity to light earlier. Ensuring an outside, independent audit each year might have as well. Board members must take firm action to see that appropriate controls are in place, insisting on specific written policies and procedures. The board is responsible for making sure that the organization has a code of conduct for all employees and a clear conflict-of-interest policy and code of ethics. It should see to it that there is only one style of financial statements used for budgeting, financial reporting, and external audit reports, allowing board members to better understand financial activity. The treasurer and finance committee should review the interim financial statements monthly (or at least quarterly in small organizations).

What to do now: With a sudden staff change and inevitable buzz surrounding the troublesome situation, it is important for the board to communicate with the rest of the staff. They must be careful not to share too many details regarding the activity, but address the issue enough to squash inaccurate rumors, answer questions, and acknowledge concerns.

In addition to having clear policies and safeguards, a prudent board should always be forthcoming with legal information. Even after an act of fraud is discovered, some nonprofits fail to go public with the information for fear that negative publicity could ruin the organization. This response may actually encourage fraud: Other individuals might believe they have a free hand to take liberties. And, there is no guarantee that a leak to the public won't occur and then the organization will be caught in a cover-up, causing an even greater upheaval in the community. Any criminal act must be reported.

Finally, it is essential for the board to take care *not* to overreact. While it is the board's responsibility to do everything possible to address the situation and ensure sound internal controls in the future, the tendency to clamp down into micromanagement and ultimately diminish the organization's ability to operate should be avoided.

A WORD ABOUT ETHICS

Jeffrey Defries, Assistant Director of The Science Museum in London, England, offers the following:

"Nonprofits must observe the highest standards in order to retain the trust of the donating public and the confidence of those they seek to help. The board provides the public face of the organization, and its behavior, and that of individual board members [as well as chief executives] must be exemplary. The issue of ethical conduct in nonprofit and public institutions is of concern to organizations and individuals worldwide. [A commitment to] key values can provide a framework for any board's [or organization's] code of ethics: Selflessness, Integrity, Objectivity, Accountability, Honesty, and Leadership."

Boards may find that discovering unethical behavior in their chief executive actually tests their own values and ethical behaviors; therefore having a discussion about code of ethics for the organization as a whole would be a worthwhile exercise leading to necessary clarification, increased understanding, and the development of consensus. Unethical behavior is not always unlawful behavior and therefore, may be more subjective than one may assume.

The repercussions of unethical behaviors should be clearly established and communicated. If a chief executive exhibits unethical behaviors, particularly after they have been informed of the organizational standards and expectations, a board will be empowered to move forward in a decisive manner to deal with that breach.

SECTION 5

MANAGEMENT STYLE AND PERSONAL ISSUES

Perhaps the most challenging aspect of managing the board–chief executive relationship is when troublesome chief executive behaviors are of a more interpersonal nature. What to do when staff members start to contact the board directly about their concerns? What if it is evident that the chief executive is a bully? What about when a chief executive is having a personal meltdown? These are some of the issues that are addressed in this section.

#20: STAFF IS COMING DIRECTLY TO THE BOARD WITH CONCERNS

What's wrong: The staff goes above the chief executive's head and directly contacts individual board members or the board as a whole with ideas or concerns either about the organization or about the chief executive.

Why this is a problem: The chief executive has accountability to the board for the management and supervision (sometimes delegated to other staff members) of the entire staff. Organizations are most effective when this delineation is observed. This does not mean that other staff members cannot interact with board members, but rather that staff concerns about the organization and its management should be addressed through the proper channels. If staff members are ignoring these channels, it may indicate that they lack faith in the leadership of the chief executive, or that the organizations lack proper procedures for staff to express concerns.

Case: Clair Newsome was a lawyer who was new to the board of the local zoo. The zoo was a gem in an otherwise small community — it was very large and highly complex, offering a multitude of community programs. Shortly after coming onto the board, Newsome found herself receiving calls from several of the VPs of the zoo — people she knew in other contexts in the community. They were very unhappy; they complained that the chief executive was driving them crazy with a management style that was extremely hands-on and lacking in people skills. Also, it seemed like every other week the board was receiving an announcement bidding a staff member farewell. "The Departed" included four of the five VPs, as well as a few directors. Newsome decided to bring it up with the chief executive in a private talk after a board meeting, and the chief executive took her comments personally, stating that she was just trying to do the best job she could.

What could have been done differently: A discussion during the hiring process about shared values and the preferred organizational culture could suggest and actually set expectations for how employees are to be treated and managed. And it is a best practice for a board of directors to adopt adequate and up-to-date human resources policies that have been vetted by outside counsel. Policies such as this often provide a statement of values. However, this situation is complicated. It is often difficult for board members to know what is actually happening inside an organization. There may be performance issues with the staff that the chief executive is working to change, or perhaps the chief executive believes the performance of an individual or a group requires a more hands-on management approach. In many cases, the board needs to honor the authority of the chief executive and leave him or her to do the job that he or she was hired to do.

At the same time, the board cannot ignore the possibility that there are issues with a challenging or inappropriate chief executive management style. In this case, the new board member should have informed the board chair of the situation. Depending on the relationships and dynamics within the organization, the board chair then might have gently probed the chief executive about his or her relationships with staff. If appropriate, the board chair could have mentioned that there is an impression that the VPs are uncomfortable and frustrated. The chair also could offer to coach the chief executive (or, with board consensus, advocate that the chief executive retain an executive coach) to handle these challenges if the chief executive is open to it.

What to do now: Sometimes a chief executive just doesn't have an awareness of how he or she is perceived by others. One way to assist with the chief executive's professional development would be to include a 360 Degree Evaluation (see sidebar). A process such as this allows the chief executive to gain unattributable feedback from staff. In these types of situations, the board also has an opportunity and a responsibility to ensure that there are grievance procedures in the human resources policies and a whistleblower policy for the red-flagging of serious organizational issues.

At some point, the board also should remind staff that the chief executive is accountable for management and supervision of the staff and organizational operations. The board should make clear that staff concerns about the organization should be addressed using appropriate internal avenues.

However, turnover can be costly. Management theory suggests that if employees are satisfied in their jobs and if other factors are in place (e.g., a positive and safe working environment, career opportunities, adequate compensation, a strong organizational culture, and the recognition of the value of one's work), employees can be encouraged not only to stay but also to excel. Every board should indicate its expectations for the chief executive to create a positive working environment that would decrease the potential for high staff turnover. Also, when trying to assess the cause of high turnover, a board, through the board chair, can take the following steps:

a) Have a candid conversation with the chief executive about the board's observations and concerns.

b) Analyze attrition by looking at turnover reports as broken down by department, supervisor, reason given for leaving, age, gender, and length of service.

c) Conduct an organization-wide satisfaction survey and ask for a review of any past surveys in order to have a benchmark.

d) Request exit interviews with staff members who have left the organization.

NECESSARY KNOWLEDGE
360 DEGREE EVALUATION INSTRUMENT

A 360 Degree Evaluation Instrument is a tool that can be used to achieve global feedback about your work performance. It is also commonly called 360 feedback, multi-source feedback, multi-rater assessment, upward feedback, or peer evaluation. Basically, each of these terms describes the process in which you evaluate yourself on a set of criteria, your manager evaluates you, as do your peers and direct reports. You receive a gap analysis detailing how you perceive yourself versus how others perceive you. Usually, following such a review, one-on-one coaching sessions are utilized to guide the development process.

Different instruments focus on different things, but the type of information that can be covered in a 360 Degree Evaluation includes:

- knowledge — familiarity with job, industry, company
- skills — task proficiency
- behaviors — patterns in relating to the environment (energy, optimism)

Personality traits or styles are generally not covered in a 360 Degree Evaluation.

The benefits of a 360 Degree Evaluation are not only to the individual, but also to that individual's team and organization. The benefits to an individual include

- helping the individual to understand how he/she is perceived by others
- helping the individual to understand developmental needs
- helping the individual to learn
- helping the individual better manage his or her own performance and career

To the individual's team and organization, the benefits include

- helping to increase communication between team members
- helping to support teamwork by involving team members in the development process
- providing better career development for employees
- working toward promotion from within
- driving organizational training considerations

#21: BULLYING OR DISPLAYING A CONTROLLING PERSONALITY

What's wrong: The chief executive has an obsessive and inappropriate need to control other people or situations and acts in a domineering, intimidating, or threatening manner in order to get his or her way.

Why this is a problem: Bullying or controlling behavior causes ill will and can compromise relationships, leading to a breakdown of trust and an inability to work together. By stifling the opinions and input of others, people acting in this way alienate fellow board members and staff from group processes. Board members, staff members, and other stakeholders begin to feel they are working for the *individual* rather than the organization and cause that brought them there in the first place. A chief executive with a controlling personality causes the organization to miss out on the knowledge and insight of other board members and staff, making potentially passive stewards of once-engaged stakeholders.

Case: Mark Connolly was the new board chair of a very large, very well-established national organization. When he became chair, he was fairly new to the board and was flattered to be asked. When it was announced that he would be serving as the chair, Connolly was told, "You'll never get anything done." It wasn't long before Connolly understood what that comment meant. Jay Redmond had been with the organization for over 12 years and had served as the chief executive for the past nine. The board was run by Redmond — he handpicked each and every incoming board member, assigned them to committees, chose the chairs, and was present at every committee meeting.

Connolly was soon faced with a major challenge. It was time for the annual chief executive performance review. Right before the meeting, Redmond told Connolly that he had already provided a written report of his accomplishments for the past year to the Personnel Committee, researched comparable salaries, and, for the convenience of the board, made the recommendation regarding his salary. Connolly had experience with human resources in the corporate sector and was quite surprised by this. Yet, when Connolly mentioned that this wasn't the way the process should happen, Redmond insisted that that this was how it always was and this is what the board expected. Connolly felt that he needed to stand firm and revisit the process. The discussion was tabled.

It was clear that the Personnel Committee was staffed completely by Redmond's champions. He would tell them what to say and wrote their reports. While there were processes and policies in place, they were carefully designed to keep the status quo. In Connolly's opinion, these policies undermined the authority of the board. When Connolly raised his concerns, it was like a dam had broken. Most members of the Executive Committee (none of whom served as members of the Personnel

Committee) agreed with Connolly and stated their objections to the process. As a committee that worked closely with Redmond, they had concerns about Redmond's past and current performance, but they had never felt empowered to raise them.

As the board began the hard conversations about best practices, it became a board divided. Redmond actively rallied his supporters, accusing Connolly of being disruptive to the organization. It was a tense, dysfunctional time for the board. Redmond was at every discussion, trying to impose his process and claiming "this is the way it has always been done."

Finally, the board agreed on a new assessment process. It utilized an anonymous online survey so that board members could be candid. They invited feedback from trustees, key staff, and important stakeholders. The input was enlightening. For the first time, the board as a whole began to see that Redmond's performance was more of an issue than originally thought — there was an undeniable awareness that while Redmond might have been a good steward for the organization in the past, he was the wrong leader to move the organization ahead for the next 10 years. After some time for reflection, the board came to the conclusion that Redmond was just not the right fit for the organization now. The board then met with Redmond and began an honest dialogue with him about what the organization needed.

"Can you believe it — this whole thing took us a full year," said an exasperated Connolly.

What could have been done differently: If the board had been composed of individuals who had experience in and a commitment to effective board governance and chief executive management rather than one with such a large contingent of individuals who had been brought onto the board by Redmond, things might have moved along more constructively. Many board members felt that they needed to be loyal to him, and in their minds that translated to being loyal to the organization.

Sometimes a board has an opportunity to be more strategic and take slow action with a longer view to address certain situations. By building board capacity first and then addressing the issues, the process may have been less painful. This could involve bringing on new board members who are more experienced, so that dealing with this issue comes from a place of enlightenment, or providing some educational or professional development segments for board members to increase their understanding of board governance. Taking it out of the personal as much as possible was what was required here.

What to do now: The board has done the heavy lifting. Now, the process of selecting a new chief executive needs to stem from a clear understanding of the type of leader that the organization needs. In addition, the board needs to reflect on the nature of its role in the future so that it does not fall into the same patterns of behavior that it exhibited under Redmond's tenure.

NECESSARY KNOWLEDGE
TEAM THEORY

One of the best ways to get the best from your chief executive is to recognize that the board and the chief executive are a team. Being part of a team requires commitment to group work. It warrants a special understanding of group dynamics and often a control of certain behaviors for the betterment of the team. When board members commit to board service, they also commit to group work, or teamwork, with the chief executive holding a special status on the team. Often, trouble in an organization stems from the failure of an individual to understand his or her place on the team, or a troublesome behavior may result as a byproduct of team development. Understanding the basics of team theory can help in recognizing and resolving situational troublesome behavior.

Referring to the groundbreaking work of Bruce W. Tuckman, whenever a group of individuals gets together for a common purpose, they form a team. Tuckman's model suggests that every team goes through five developmental stages: (1) forming, (2) storming, (3) norming, (4) performing, and (5) adjourning.

While these stages can flow from one to the other, internal and external impacts might readily move a team backward or forward by one or two stages. In the context of nonprofit boards, examples of nonlinear progression may come from the addition of a new board member, a change in board leadership, a term ending or resignation of a board member, a chief executive transition, or an organizational crisis. At each stage, teams display various behaviors and team members experience different feelings. With each different feeling or behavior, the productivity of the team is affected.

#22: EXHIBITING EMOTIONAL ISSUES AND DEPENDENCY

What is wrong: When a chief executive suffers from a deeply personal issue or disease — whether it is substance abuse, depression, anxiety, the loss of a loved one, or something else.

Why is this a problem: The chief executive may not have the ability to keep her reactions to these personal problems apart from her professional life. It can deeply affect the organization, harming her ability to be of service or reflecting poorly on the organization's image.

Case: Carol Culbert had been a great volunteer for the Families and Friends of Those with Cancer Institute. She attended all the organizational events, actively brought new friends into the organization, raised money, and gave money. Culbert had been involved in the organization one way or another for years and because of this commitment and her past work experience, about a year ago she was hired as its chief executive.

Unfortunately, it was now clear that she had a drinking problem. It hadn't been a problem in the early years, and no one had a clue when she was hired. But over the past year, it seemed like her drinking was out of control. At two separate events, she became so inebriated she could barely walk. And after one, a board member had to hide her keys and call her a cab.

The funny thing was that no one talked about it. Everyone liked Culbert, but other than seeing her on the job, at events, and at meetings, no one really knew her. Board members didn't know if it was their place to say anything or do anything. It had gotten to the point where there was an unspoken pact that board members and staff would keep an eye on Culbert from the moment she arrived until she left. Some secretly feared that they would hear the next morning that she had been in a car accident.

What could have been done differently: A background or in-depth reference check may have shed some light on Culbert's drinking problem. However, it may be an issue that had recently escalated, or it may be that others would be reluctant to share information of this kind with anyone who was doing a background or reference check.

What to do now: Behavior like Culbert's can cause a string of disappointments, most likely turning into other troublesome behaviors such as lateness, absence, lack of preparedness, lack of focus or ability to concentrate in meetings, mood swings, possible unethical or illegal behavior to support a dependency, or violence. Many times work performance is impaired and other staff or board members must cover for the troubled individual, working harder because of his or her failures. As the chief executive, Culbert is the face of the organization, and her dependency problems could ultimately hurt the organization's reputation.

Serious intervention is needed. A human resources professional should be confidentially consulted to determine the best course of action.

GET THE BEST FROM YOUR CHIEF EXECUTIVE

Give your chief executive YOUR very best. When you are focused, creative, loyal, committed, and demanding of yourself in serving your organization's mission, truly talented and committed colleagues are quick to catch the fire. Great service inspires great service.

Lawrence D. P. Vellani, MPA
Board Chair
Alamance Partnership for Children

A Great Example of a Great Relationship

While this book focuses on how to manage challenging scenarios, the author would be remiss in not acknowledging the thousands of cases where the board–chief executive relationship is strong, vibrant, and productive. It is a constant journey dedicated to the building, maintaining, and honoring human relationships.

Marilyn Alexander is a member of the board of governors of Chapman University in California. She relates the following story:

Chapman University is a small private university founded in 1861. Its current president has been there for a significant amount of time and his relationship with our board is just fabulous.

About 20 years ago, the University was in very bad financial shape. Applications and enrollments were down and the financial picture was bleak. The board named Jim Doti as the interim president for a year. Jim had been an economics professor at Chapman. A new president was hired; it wasn't a good fit. The board turned to Jim once again and ultimately made him the permanent president.

If you were to see the statistics on what we've been able accomplish in the last 15 years, you would think they were too good to be true. On a line graph, you would see in every area a sharp rise at a 45-degree angle. Through hard work the University has made progress in every measurable area.

Time, Treasure, Talent. Our board has consistently given all three. They walked the talk. If you walked around the campus, you would see the names of our board members on buildings that they have funded. And Jim inspired that.

Our board meetings are run like a very well-run corporate board. Each board member is incredibly involved.

If I had the opportunity to share what I have learned from my experience at Chapman and comparing it with what I have seen at other organizations, this is what stands out. Chief executives have to get the message that boards are not a necessary evil. This is so incredibly demotivating. They also need to use the talent and expertise that board members bring to the table. The best chief executives check their ego at the door. Chief executives need to get over themselves so that they can really use their boards.

SECTION 6

THE BASICS: GETTING THE BEST FROM YOUR CHIEF EXECUTIVE

Getting the best from your chief executive is a process that starts when an organization first begins its discussions with a prospective hire. Many of the challenging behaviors and difficult situations explored in the previous pages are often the result of boards not following the right procedures in hiring and orientation.

Has the board thought through the specific requirements of the position and developed a clear job description? Does the organization have clear policies delineating the authorities that are vested in the chief executive? Has the board paid enough attention to the orientation of the chief executive and the need to create a productive and welcoming work environment for its new hire?

Addressing these questions can help the board reduce the likelihood of problems down the line. (BoardSource has numerous resources for boards on hiring issues; see the Suggested Resources section for more details.) But even with the best hiring and orientation policies in place, organizations cannot entirely avoid resulting difficult situations. In fact, it is a rare organization that does not face challenges in the relationship between a board and its chief executive at some point. The remainder of this book takes a closer look at many of the specific challenges that can arise, and at how boards can respond most effectively.

THE SEARCH PROCESS AND THE BOARD'S RESPONSIBILITY FOR DUE DILIGENCE

Depending upon the size and complexity of the organization, determining whether or not to engage professional help for a search requires the weighing of the specific pros and cons. Some nonprofits simply can't afford to do so, and some nonprofits have their own human resources departments and therefore don't need to do so. However, a search may or may not be a commitment best served by a staff member, who has other responsibilities, or by a volunteer board member that also has other responsibilities, and likely holds a full-time job in addition to board service. There are also the hours a search committee spends in conference calls, meetings, and interviews, as well as other staff hours to support the search, and utilizing an outside professional may provide a desired economy of scale.

And regardless of how the search is undertaken, it is important to recognize that while there are no guarantees that anyone you hire will be with an organization for life, boards need to look at hiring the next chief executive with all the hopes and dreams of entering into a lifelong marriage. This sets up the new chief executive with all the potential for success, and it also minimizes any disastrous results of a poor hire. Hiring poorly has hidden but very real costs — some estimate that it is not uncommon for the costs of top level position turnover to be 100–150 percent of that person's annual salary, because of recruitment costs, interview expenses, training, and possible interim contract support. It could, of course, be much higher. The search for a chief executive is also extremely time-consuming. It is estimated that a comprehensive chief executive search can take up to 200 hours over a three-to-six month period to steward.

Briefly, the steps in the chief executive search process may include the following:

- interviewing board members, staff, and other key stakeholders to determine organizational need and readiness

- reviewing and revising the job description

- establishing the salary and compensation package

- appropriate advertising and use of formal and informal professional networking channels to attract candidates by a stated deadline

- receiving résumés and screening them against agreed-upon criteria (i.e., the job description)

- determining an initial pool of candidates, generally between 10 and 15 candidates

- asking the initial pool to provide additional information such as answers to a standard set of written questions

- determining the final pool of candidates, generally between three and six candidates

- conducting a predefined interview process (who will participate, what questions will be asked, use of a decision matrix)

- extending and negotiating the offer, which includes a discussion of board expectations and policies and the evaluation process

- arranging for a meeting with key staff

- conducting reference and background checks

It is very important for the board to determine in advance of the hire a reasonable compensation package for the incoming chief executive. Many boards make the mistake of just going with "whatever has been budgeted" or "whatever the last chief executive was making" and while these amounts may be appropriate, it is the board's responsibility to ensure that due diligence regarding appropriate compensation prior to the hire. For example:

> *I know of a situation where a founding chief executive is now looking at retirement. She is concerned that her board does not understand that the salary she has been making is not competitive in today's market. For years, because of her personal circumstances and her commitment to the organization, she had scrimped and saved and made recommendations that kept her salary at a certain level. This also had the result of keeping other staff salaries down. Because of their enormous respect for her, the board just went along with her recommendations. This board is in for a huge wake-up call — it has not kept its collective eyes and ears open to the external environment.*

or

> *We really didn't know what hit us. We went through the process and were so excited — we found just the right person for the job. But when we extended the offer, he wanted twice what we were offering — twice what the last chief executive was making! Half of the board wanted to give him what he asked for. The other half were vehemently against this. It delayed the hire and put us in crisis mode for quite some time while we sorted out what was the right thing to do. Ultimately, we lost him as a candidate and had to start again from scratch.*

Comparing compensation against similar organizations is part of the board's due diligence. This can be done by doing your own research or by using an outside consulting firm to produce a salary comparison report. When comparing organizations that are similar in budget and staff size, industry/programs/services, and geographic location, information to consider includes base salary, health/life insurance, retirement plans, leave policies, etc. The board should ensure that chief executive compensation has been determined through a process that benchmarks such compensation against established comparables. A written report of this process should be kept as part of the chief executive's personnel file.

NECESSARY KNOWLEDGE

SAMPLE CHIEF EXECUTIVE JOB DESCRIPTION KEY COMPONENTS

Position Title
Classification
Salary Grade
Annual Leave at Hire
Reports to
Primary Relationships
Direct Reports
Objective
Essential Functions, Duties, and Responsibilities
• Leadership/Management
• Official Spokesperson
• Strategic Direction
• Business Planning
• Financial Planning
• Sustainability (Revenue Generation & Fundraising)
• Talent Management/Team-Building
• External Relationship Building
• Compliance
• Board of Directors Relationship
Qualification Requirements
Position Expectations
Work Environment
Acknowledgments

HIRING: GETTING THE RIGHT CANDIDATE FOR THE RIGHT REASONS

"I really liked her warmth."

"He is so articulate — he really knows what he is talking about."

"She is completely different from the last chief executive. And we all know how challenging that was. We just need a change."

"My friend said that she did a great job in her last position."

[Thinking to herself] *"Not it. If we hire this candidate, I know he will make sure that the new reading program is instituted — the last chief executive kept saying it wasn't consistent with our mission and that we didn't have the resources to effectively do this. But this is why I came on this board — to get this up and running!"*

© 2009 BoardSource

Sometimes boards make selections for the wrong reasons. They hire for personality or based on personal agendas, or they hire on the basis of someone else's strong recommendation without seeking out additional information or conducting reference checks. However, using a clearly outlined process informed by clearly defined organizational needs, and applied equally to all candidates, will usually allow the best to rise to the top for board consideration as well as serve the board's governance responsibility.

And sometimes boards simply don't complete the critical last steps in the hiring process. Conducting background checks (both criminal and credit) can bring a lot of information to the table. Such information is now readily available and to not take advantage of the available resources might be considered a fiduciary abdication.

PROPER ONBOARDING AND ORIENTATION

Onboarding is a term that means properly introducing, orienting, installing, and welcoming someone into organizational culture. It refers to both formal and informal processes and requires being actively sensitive to the fact that a new job for anyone is a major life transition fraught with excitement coupled with a measure of anxiety. In response to proper onboarding, turnover is reduced and restructuring is more successful. The term is actually used more in the corporate sector than in the nonprofit sector. Onboarding is most often used in the context of teamwork theory and in understanding the need to move to the productive stage quickly when new teams are formed or existing teams experience a transition. (For more information see the sidebar on Team Theory on p. 48.)

Anytime a person joins or leaves an organization, a group dynamic shift takes place. Proper onboarding of the chief executive is an often overlooked but necessary part of board work *and* it actively helps to prevent challenges in the board–chief executive relationship from beginning. Sometimes boards make the mistake of leaving the process of onboarding to staff, or even expecting the new chief executive to onboard him- or herself. In addition to a formal orientation, using a "New Hire Checklist" will help to ensure that the chief executive is fully supported administratively by the time he or she starts the job.

NECESSARY KNOWLEDGE
SAMPLE ORIENTATION SCHEDULE

TOPIC	BY WHOM
Review history and mission	Board and Staff
Review of governance structure and practices	Board
Strategic plan and resulting operational plans and staff	Board and Staff
Organizational culture and staff	Board and Staff
Review of organizational chart	Staff
Human Resources policy highlights and benefits	Staff
Review of job description and responsibilities	Board
Review of goals and performance review process	Board
Management information system and office management	Staff
Financial management and accounting	Staff
Legal	Staff
Program/Service Delivery departments	Staff
Communications — internal and external	Staff
Public policy	Board and Staff
Key external relationships	Board and Staff
Staff introductions	Board and Staff

Providing a positive work environment is another important aspect of ensuring that the chief executive's tenure gets off on the right foot. It's amazing what a pleasant office with organized files and working equipment can do to motivate and support new employees.

CONFIRMING WHO'S THE BOSS

Successful chief executives understand that they serve a board, clients and other stakeholders, and employees. They have to balance the needs and interests of all these constituencies in order to create and maintain organizational progress and success. However, the chief executive does have a "boss" — the board of directors. Successful boards understand that the board selects and supervises the chief executive through unified consensus, i.e., it speaks with one voice, generally through the board chair–chief executive relationship. The board supports its chief executive by providing him or her with frequent and constructive informal feedback, and by annually conducting a formal performance evaluation to help the chief executive strengthen his or her performance. Somewhere in the middle are naturally varied perspectives and definitions of the latitude of behavior and practice. People may have honest differences of opinion about style, how to get from "A" to "B," or about the way to measure success. Having frequent and candid conversations about this during the hiring and onboarding processes can help to prevent misunderstandings in the relationship as well as build trust.

DELEGATION OF AUTHORITY

In addition to a well-written job description, ensuring board consensus about the delineation of authority and delegation to a chief executive can help to prevent common relationship breakdowns in the future. Board members should review, discuss, revise, and, if necessary, develop written policies that govern the duties of the chief executive *before* the hire to ensure that the board is providing a new chief executive with a clear understanding of the standards and expectations of performance. For an example of a formal board delegation of authority to a chief executive, please see the Appendix.

CHIEF EXECUTIVE BURNOUT

Good hiring and orientation practices are key to retaining good leaders. In the groundbreaking study *Daring to Lead 2006: A National Study of Nonprofit Executive Leadership*, a joint project of CompassPoint Nonprofit Services and The Meyer Foundation, we find the following:

- *Executives who are unhappy with their boards are more than twice as likely to be planning near-term departures as those who have positive perceptions of their boards.*

- *Only one in three executives agrees strongly that their board challenges them in ways that make them more effective.*

- *Only one in three executives agrees strongly that their staff view the board as an engaged leadership body.*

- *Only one in three executives agrees strongly that their funders have a good understanding of the nonprofit executive job.*

ESTABLISHING A PROPER CHIEF EXECUTIVE EVALUATION

While most boards fully understand their responsibility and role to annually evaluate their chief executive, few boards understand that they have an opportunity to determine the specifics of the evaluation process in advance of the chief executive hire. By doing so, the board's recruitment can be much more effective because it will be done through the lens of the specific needs of the organization at that time. It also helps to inform the chosen incoming candidate of the clarified and shared expectations of the board.

In general, a proper chief executive evaluation process would include four key sections:

- evaluation of annual performance goals

- evaluation of core competencies

- evaluation of leadership qualities

- evaluation of accomplishments and challenges

Developing a collective board vision for the annual performance goals of the incoming chief executive also serves to develop a unified message regarding organizational priorities from the board to the chief executive. There is then little chance for the new chief executive to not know what his or her charge is upon hire. These clarifications also serve as a foundation that a board can refer to in the future.

As noted in BoardSource's 2006 publication *Taming the Troublesome Board Member* by this author, utilizing standard constructive ways to give feedback to a chief executive can make or break an evaluation process. This book deals with many difficult situations that can arise in the relationship between the board and the chief executive. Most often, the first step in addressing these situations is to initiate a conversation about the problems that the board is perceiving. By meeting with the chief executive, the board chair and/or responsible committee can clarify perceptions, develop options for resolution, solicit the chief executive's understanding and agreement to a course of action, and plan for follow up afterwards to ensure a successful resolution for all.

Giving and receiving feedback takes conscious effort and can be most successful if those involved understand that some simple ground rules will make all the difference in the world.

When *giving* feedback:

- Ask if you can give feedback and if it's the right time. Honor the answer.
- State your intention as to why you wish to give feedback.
- Plan your words and your tone.
- Ask if the person has any questions or responses and then *listen*.
- Set up a future time to continue the discussion if necessary.
- Respect the person for hearing you out.
- Thank the person for listening.

So, how can one say something that should be obvious without letting the chief executive think he or she is being insulted?

- Be descriptive rather than evaluative. By repeating what you understood the other person to say without evaluating the content, the speaker is reassured that he or she is being listened to and understood.
- Be specific. By citing examples of specific behavior, the individual will better understand how he or she acted in a way that is triggering this conversation and how the situation might be avoided in the future.
- Focus on the feelings of the person who has experienced the behavior and is offering the feedback. By using the "I" language rather than making accusations about the other person (or using the royal "we" as in, "everybody feels this way…"), the person giving feedback prevents automatic, defensive responses and increases the likelihood that his or her point will be considered. It is difficult to challenge a statement about how someone feels.

- Direct the conversation at elements of the behavior the receiver can do something about. Only feedback that has the potential to solicit a change in behavior is constructive.

- Time it well. Feedback can be ineffective if tempers are too high or the current situation had degenerated beyond salvage. Time your feedback so that it is given when it is least threatening.

- Check to ensure clear communication. Ending feedback with a summation of the conversation ensures that you have made your point clearly and that the individual understands how his or her behavior affects the group.

- Avoid "dumping" or "unloading" on the other person. Feedback is not a venting process; it is designed to help the individual make positive changes in his or her behavior. Feedback used to "get something off your chest" is rarely effective and may alienate the recipient.

- Don't ask, "Why?" It is not effective to ask someone why they act in a certain way — often, they won't know. It is better to focus on the future and how the behavior can be improved.

And remember that when one provides feedback it should never be thought of as a one-way conversation. There is an opportunity to see things from someone else's perspective and the giver should be open to receiving feedback as well. When receiving feedback

- Be sure you are in the right frame of mind to hear what's being offered. If not, set another time that would be better.

- Listen (active listening) and breathe deeply to keep yourself calm and focused.

- Respect the other person for offering the feedback.

- Ask clarifying questions to increase your understanding of what is being offered.

- Resist the impulse to defend at this time. Take time to think about what you've heard.

- Don't disagree — there may be an ounce of truth that you must consider before responding.

- Schedule a time to reconvene and finish the discussion.

- Thank the person for giving the feedback.

Ultimately, of course, learning from the conversation and deriving preventative strategies can reduce the risk of encountering similar situations in the future.

PUNITIVE EVALUATIONS

Sadly, because they see no other way out, many boards attempt to correct (or even end) a bad board–chief executive relationship through a punitive performance evaluation process. Ideally, a performance evaluation should focus on the future and be designed to improve chief executive performance. While performance evaluations do, at times, include a factual documentation of challenging performance issues, they should emphasize what the chief executive can do going forward. Using information about past action can and should certainly inform the process, but a performance evaluation is designed to increase effectiveness by setting goals for additional professional development and furthering organizational goals.

The board can use the process to identify goals for the coming year and discuss how the chief executive can best achieve them. Feedback throughout the year as well as in this process should not shame or punish but rather can help illustrate where performance might be less than desired and create the opportunity to strategize on steps for improvement. Look to the past with the goal of learning and encouraging how one might increase performance.

CONCLUSION
WE'RE ONLY HUMAN

If I could be you, if you could be me
For just one hour, if we could find a way
To get inside each other's mind
If you could see you through my eyes
Instead of your own ego I believe you'd be
Surprised to see
That you've been blind
Walk a mile in my shoes
Just walk a mile in my shoes
Before you abuse, criticize and accuse
Walk a mile in my shoes

Elvis Presley hit (words and music by Joe South)

A book like this would not be written unless with the following caveat: While we recognize that challenging board–chief executive relationships *do* exist and *will* interfere with the effectiveness and potential success of a nonprofit organization, the identification of the problem must be one with an end goal of seeking to understand that problem while offering possible solutions. The world would be better for all if everyone's work began with an attempt to build bridges instead of walls and an understanding that, on a fundamental level, we are all connected. It is important to look at this issue from a humanistic perspective. Behaviors are behaviors and people are people. Label the behavior, not the person.

The first step toward understanding and appropriately dealing with troublesome behaviors is to actively use the Golden Rule. It is best interpreted as saying: Treat others the way you'd like to be treated. If you act in a given way toward someone, yet are unwilling to be treated that way in the same circumstances, then you violate the rule. A little understanding mixed with a little awareness of our effects on others can go a long way.

HOLDING UP THE MIRROR

As shown with many of the solutions and conversation starters, most times all it takes is for the board to reach out to the chief executive and help him into realization. If an individual doesn't realize that he or she is offending or debilitating someone or something, it can't be corrected.

The initial strategy should always be to address directly, counsel, and coach for better behavior. Sometimes one finds that there is more to the behavior than someone just being difficult. It could be a chief executive in good conscience trying to bring up an elephant in the room. He or she could have a sincere concern about an organizational situation, condition, or consequence that may not be seen or dealt with by others. Or this person may be intentionally taking on the devil's advocate role, which can be a positive thing unless it is abused (intentionally or unintentionally) and expends too much time and energy by overchallenging the group consensus at every meeting. And again, it may just be that someone is just not aware that his or her behaviors are viewed as problematic, especially when it is a pattern of behavior no one has ever addressed before or because the individual has no other frame of reference.

Sometimes even after doing all of the preventative work and/or attempting the solutions that have been discussed, an individual just may not be able to effectively work as a team member or function in an appropriate manner within the context of the board–chief executive relationship. The kicker is: Personality and ego come into play in nonprofit work in the same way they do in families, clubs, businesses, and other teams or group formations. If it isn't situational acting out, it could be just the wrong team/fit, or it could be a permanent character flaw.

GOOD NIGHT AND GOOD LUCK

After all that's been said, it may just be that a chief executive who is not measuring up should simply be asked to step down. The stated attributes of a written annual assessment process and a removal mechanism clearly stated in the hire is highly advantageous so that someone who isn't living up to expectations can be removed. If the conditions under which removal will be considered are spelled out and communicated in advance and then applied consistently, it becomes a reflective group process rather than a real or perceived personal indictment.

If there is a special situation in which a chief executive's behaviors are challenging to the point of prompting action in between annual reviews, the board should convene in a timely manner to address the issue and make the recommendation for removal. If the chief executive has committed an illegal or otherwise highly serious infraction, the board should not wait but act immediately and swiftly. If the issue is incompetence and no remedies have worked to bring about improvement, the board should cut its losses and proceed to suggest resignation or remove the chief executive.

The last resort would be a vote for removal. This is necessary when the chief executive's behavior has been so egregious that keeping him or her in the seat would be against the organization's best interests and/or put the organization in financial or legal jeopardy. Or, after a fair chance for understanding and change was given to the chief executive, he or she didn't do anything to alter the behavior. Again, this determination should be made with deliberation and due process. An executive session could take place *without* the presence of the chief executive and then the full board must vote on the final decision for removal. In this event, plans for organizational continuity should be well discussed in advance of any action taken by the board.

The new discoveries (and resulting wonders) in quantum mechanics encourage each of us to think in terms of unfathomable possibilities. Many believe there is another major paradigm shift ahead for the human race. This shift will include a greater understanding and knowledge that we are all connected, that we are all one, and that life is eternal — an unprecedented melding of science and spirituality. That everything each of us thinks, does, or says, positive or negative, has an impact on the rest of us — a state of mutual coexistence for all time.

Could the historic role of philanthropy and serving nonprofits be one of the stepping stones on the road to this paradigm shift? Do we (should we) give to live? Does the emotion of compassion exist so that we can eventually understand how truly connected we all are?

Working and living well requires meaning. There are few things as satisfying as using one's talents, skills, and experience to serve the public good. Yet, as Brian L. Weiss, M.D., says in his book *Many Lives, Many Masters* (Simon and Schuster, 1988), "...experience is necessary to add emotional belief to intellectual understanding." It all comes down to human interaction and the building of relationships.

Wouldn't it be nice if someday, the need for formal philanthropy, the existence of nonprofit organizations, the giving of the haves to the have-nots, would not be necessary? Would not even be in the human frame of reference? That this could be so because our relationships with one another, stranger and friend, were strong, healthy, and compassionate?

Figuring out the cause of board–chief executive relationship challenges in any context starts with compassion and understanding. Add some gentleness and kindness when addressing the conflicts and we will all be closer to honoring the primary law of peaceful coexistence.

May it be so.

APPENDIX

GRANTING AUTHORITY TO THE CHIEF EXECUTIVE: A TEMPLATE

Boards have an opportunity to state specifically, in writing, the specific delegations of authority they are granting to the chief executive. Such a statement then provides a basis for the chief executive's accountability to the board.

The late George Knight, a board member of NEIGHBORWORKS® AMERICA, provided the following example:

- Manage the day-to-day affairs of the organization as its chief executive.

- Provide financial reports to the Board and/or its appropriate committee(s) on no less than a quarterly basis.

- Implement the organization's strategic planning process and establish new programs, consistent with the mission, in consultation with the Board of Directors.

- Develop and submit annual budgets for approval by a specific date annually based on operational plans stemming from the strategic plan.

- Provide monthly dashboard reports of organizational progress against stated goals to the Board and/or appropriate committee(s) as defined.

- Arrange for tax payments or other government ordered payments or filings to be paid in a timely and accurate manner.

- Select, employ, fix the compensation and benefits of, and remove employees, according to both law and the established board-approved human resources policies; and to settle payroll and debts in a timely manner.

- Select and contract with consultants and professional services contractors as budgeted and as necessary.

- Approve and execute applications and/or renewal forms related to charitable solicitation as required in states where the organization registers to raise funds under charitable solicitation statutes.

- Establish, and as necessary amend, organizational charts and administrative practices and procedures for efficient and effective operation.

- Lead the organization's fundraising/sponsorship activities in accordance with established organizational policies.

- Lead the organization's program or service delivery activities in accordance with established organizational policies.

- Arrange for the appropriate levels of insurance against theft and casualty losses to at least __ percent replacement value and against liability losses to board members, staff, and the organization itself in an amount greater than the average for comparable organizations.

- Establish comprehensive organizational emergency and disaster preparedness plans.

- Arrange, through purchase, lease, grant, or otherwise for offices, furniture, equipment, and facilities, including the authority to execute all office and facility leases, up to $_____ and to seek approval for same for any agreements over $_____.

- Negotiate and execute contracts and other agreements committing the organization to the receipt or disposition of assets, or to the acquisition, holding, or disposition of any property, consistent with the organization's mission up to $_____ and to seek approval for same for any agreements over $_____.

- Approve and execute all grants without limitation, consistent with the organizational mission, and provide a report on all grants awarded to the board or its appropriate committee(s) on a quarterly basis.

- Establish, from time to time, amend, and enforce the terms and conditions under which agreements are made.

- Serve as the organization's official spokesperson and delegate this responsibility as deemed appropriate and necessary.

- Complain for or defend the organization, or otherwise represent its interests, in any judicial or legislative proceedings that may affect its purposes or operations.

- Upon formal or informal request or invitation, appear before, meet, confer, or consult regarding the organization or its mission area with members, committees, or subcommittees of Congress and their professional staffs or any other legislative body; but to ensure that no part of the organization's activities shall be used to contribute to or otherwise support any candidate for elective public office.

- Settle, adjust, and compromise any claim, demand, right of, by or against, the organization; exercise such other authority as may be necessary and proper to carry out the authorities granted by the Board.

- Delegate any or all of such authorities to other officers or employees of the organization, provided that each such delegation or re-delegation is: (a) in writing; (b) signed by the chief executive; and (c) consistent with any board policy.

SUGGESTED RESOURCES

American Bar Association Committee on Nonprofit Governance. *Guide to Nonprofit Corporate Governance in the Wake of Sarbanes-Oxley.* Chicago: American Bar Association, 2006.

Bell, Jeanne, Richard Moyers, and Timothy Wolfred. *Daring to Lead 2006: A National Study of Nonprofit Leadership.* A Joint Project of CompassPoint Nonprofit Services and The Meyer Foundation.

Blanchard, Kenneth, and Norman Vincent Peale. *The Power of Ethical Management.* New York, NY, William Morrow, 1988.

BoardSource. *Board Self-Assessment: Assess to Advance.* Washington, DC: BoardSource, 2009.

BoardSource. *The Nonprofit Board Answer Book, Second Edition.* San Francisco: Jossey-Bass, 2008.

BoardSource. *The Source: Twelve Principles of Governance That Power Exceptional Boards.* Washington, DC: BoardSource, 2005.

Butler, Lawrence M. *The Nonprofit Dashboard: A Tool for Tracking Progress.* Washington, DC: BoardSource, 2007.

Carver, John. *Boards That Make a Difference: A New Design for Leadership in Nonprofit and Public Organizations. Third Edition.* San Francisco: Jossey-Bass, 2006.

Chait, Richard P. *How to Help Your Board Govern More and Manage Less.* Washington, DC: BoardSource, 2003.

Chait, Richard P., William P. Ryan, and Barbara E. Taylor. *Governance as Leadership: Reframing the Work of Nonprofit Boards.* Hoboken, NJ: John Wiley & Sons, 2004.

Connolly, Paul M. *Navigating the Organizational Life Cycle: A Capacity Building Guide for Nonprofit Leaders.* Washington, DC: BoardSource, 2006.

Defries, Jeffrey. "A Board Member's Code of Ethics." Reprinted from the March 1998 edition of Board Member 7, no. 3 (2006).

Fichandler, Zelda. "Whither (or Wither) Art?" in *The Art of Governance: Boards in the Performing Arts,* edited by Nancy Rouche and Jaan Whitehead. New York: Theatre Communications Group, 2005.

Fisher, B. A. *Small Group Decision Making. Second Edition.* New York: McGraw-Hill, 1980.

Kissman, Katha. *Taming the Troublesome Board Member.* Washington, DC: BoardSource, 2006.

Lakey, Berit M. *The Board Building Cycle, Second Edition.* Washington, DC: BoardSource, 2007.

Lakey, Berit M., Sandra R. Hughes, and Outi Flynn. *Governance Committee.* Washington, DC: BoardSource, 2004.

Lancaster, Lynne C., and David Stillman. *When Generations Collide: Who They Are. Why They Clash. How to Solve the Generational Puzzle at Work.* New York: HarperCollins Publishers, 2002.

Lawrence, Barbara, and Outi Flynn. *The Nonprofit Policy Sampler, Second Edition.* Washington, DC: BoardSource, 2006.

Lieberman, David J. *How to Change Anybody.* New York: St. Martin's Press, 2005.

Mathiason, Gary G. *"How to Fire a CEO: Ending (Legally) the Most Important Employment Relationship for a Company."* Executive Counsel, Fall 2004.

Mintz, Joshua, and Jane Pierson. *Assessment of the Chief Executive: A Tool for NonprofitBoards, Revised.* Washington, DC: BoardSource, 2005.

Moyers, Richard L. *The Nonprofit Chief Executive's Ten Basic Responsibilities.* Washington, DC: BoardSource, 2006.

Seashore, Charles N., Edith Whitfield Seashore, and Gerald M. Weinberg. *What Did You Say? The Art of Giving and Receiving Feedback.* Columbia, MD: Bingham House Books, 1992.

Solomon, Muriel. *Working with Difficult People.* London: Prentice-Hall International (UK), 1990.

Tuckman, B. W. *"Development Sequence in Small Groups."* Psychological Bulletin, 1965, 63 (6) in Fay, Peter P. Doyle, Austin G., Stages of Group Development, University Associates.

Various Authors. *The Governance Series.* Washington, DC: BoardSource, 2009.

- Dambach, Charles, Melissa Davis, and Robert L. Gale. *Structures and Practices of Nonprofit Boards, Second Edition.* Washington, DC: BoardSource, 2009.

- Grace, Kay Sprinkel, Amy McClellan, and John A. Yankey. *The Nonprofit Board's Role in Mission, Planning, and Evaluation, Second Edition.* Washington, DC: BoardSource, 2009.

- Greenfield, James M. *Fundraising Responsibilities of Nonprofit Boards, Second Edition.* Washington, DC: BoardSource, 2009.

- Hopkins, Bruce R. *Legal Responsibilities of Nonprofit Boards, Second Edition.* Washington, DC: BoardSource, 2009.

- Ingram, Richard T. *Ten Basic Responsibilities of Nonprofit Boards, Second Edition.* Washington, DC: BoardSource, 2009.

- Lang, Andrew S. *Financial Responsibilities of Nonprofit Boards, Second Edition.* Washington, DC: BoardSource, 2009.

Wertheimer, Mindy R. *The Board Chair Handbook, Second Edition.* Washington, DC: BoardSource, 2007.

Zemke, Ron, Claire Raines, and Bob Filipczak. *Generations at Work: Managing the Clash of Veterans, Boomers, Xers, and Nexters in Your Workplace.* New York: American Management Association, 2000.

ABOUT THE AUTHOR

Katha Kissman is a BoardSource senior governance consultant. Based in the Washington, D.C. area, Kissman has over 25 years of experience managing and consulting with nonprofits. As a senior governance consultant, Kissman provides individualized board consultation and training and conducts workshops on governance issues. Kissman has worked with a variety of organizations including the Boys & Girls Club of America, Corporation for Public Broadcasting, Lincoln County Community Foundation, and LA Art, among others. She has particular expertise in assisting boards with compliance, fiscal management, fundraising, relations and retention, risk management, special events, strategic planning, team-building, and training.

In addition to providing governance consulting through BoardSource, Kissman also serves as an interim leader, providing organizations with a short- or long-term leadership bridge, and provides nonprofit organizational development consulting. Previously, she served as Leadership America's executive director in 1996 and 1997 and then again as its president and CEO in 2000 and 2001. She lived in the United Arab Emirates in 1998 and 1999 where she helped found the American University of Sharjah's Continuing Education Center. Kissman also helped found the American University of Kuwait's Continuing Education Center in 2004. In 2009, Kissman received the Linguistic Society of America's Linguistic Service Award for her service as its interim executive director.

Kissman currently serves or has served with the Office Depot Business Women's Council, IONA Senior Services, the African Continuum Theatre Company, the Trans-Arab Research Institute, the New Buffalo Railroad Museum, Leadership Montgomery, the Berrien County Economic Development Commission, the Harbor Country Chamber of Commerce, the Maryland State Arts Council, the Cultural Alliance of Greater Washington, Greentree Shelter for Women, NOW, and Hexagon.

In addition to authoring this publication, Kissman wrote *Taming the Troublesome Board Member* (available through BoardSource) in 2006. She is also a contributor to *Board Member* magazine. She received her B.S. in Public Administration, School of Public Service at Grand Valley State University in Grand Rapids, Michigan.

For further information or to contact her, please visit her Web site at www.kathakissman.com.